The History of the Holy Mar Ma'in with a Guide to the Persian Martyr Acts

Persian Martyr Acts in Syriac: Text and Translation

1

Series Editor
Adam H. Becker

Persian Martyr Acts in Syriac is a series of Syriac martyrological texts composed from the fourth century into the Islamic period. They detail the martyrdom of a diversity of Christians at the hands of Sasanian kings, bureaucrats, and priests. These documents vary from purely mythological accounts to descriptions of actual events with a clear historical basis, however distorted by the hagiographer's hand.

The History of the Holy Mar Ma'in with a Guide to the Persian Martyr Acts

Sebastian P. Brock

Gorgias Press
2008

First Gorgias Press Edition, 2008

Published in the United States of America by Gorgias Press LLC, New Jersey

ISBN 978-1-59333-222-8
ISSN 1941-871X

GORGIAS PRESS
180 Centennial Ave., Suite 3, Piscataway, NJ 08854 USA
www.gorgiaspress.com

Library of Congress Cataloging-in-Publication Data
Brock, Sebastian P.
The history of the Holy Mar Ma'in with a guide to the Persian martyr acts / Sebastian P. Brock. -- 1st Gorgias Press ed.
p. cm. -- (Persian martyr acts in Syriac : texts and translation ; v. 1)
Includes bibliographical references and indexes.
ISBN 978-1-59333-222-8 (alk. paper)
1. Ma'in, ca. 310-ca. 424. 2. Christian martyrs--Iran. 3. Martyrologies. 4. Syriac literature. I. Title.
PJ5631.B76 2008
892'.3--dc22

2008026785

The paper used in this publication meets the minimum requirements of the American National Standards.

Printed in the United States of America

TABLE OF CONTENTS

PREFACE

Whether in the fourth or in the twentieth and twenty-first century, martyrdom has at times been very much a reality for many Christians living in the geographical area of modern Iraq and western Iran, and this has been equally the case at particular periods during the course of the intervening centuries. For the most part, however, it is only for the martyrs living under Sasanian rule (AD 224–651) that written records, sometimes extensive, of these martyrdoms have been preserved.

Persecution only became a serious threat for Christians in the Persian Empire after Constantine's conversion to Christianity, and thus after the cessation of persecution within the Roman Empire. Significantly, persecution was most likely to take place in the Persian Empire during times of hostility between the two empires, and this was particularly the case in the mid fourth century, when it continued on and off during the last 35 years of the long reign of Shapur II (309–79). Indeed Shapur's reign witnessed the most extensive persecutions, resulting in a large number of deaths; the shorter bouts of persecution in the first half of the fifth century, at the end of the reign of Yazdgard I (399–420) and the beginning of the reign of Bahram V (420–38), and in that of Yazdgard II (439–57), likewise took place at times of tension between the two superpowers. By the mid fifth century, however, Christians had become an important minority within the Persian Empire, and subsequent martyrdoms were largely confined to high-profile cases of individual converts from Zoroastrianism who were of high birth.

The literary records, or Acts, of these martyrs vary enormously in character and historical value, ranging from what are little more than mere lists of names to writings with literary pretensions that have taken on a largely legendary character, though probably retaining traces of a historical core. The *History of Ma'in*, who was technically a confessor, and not a martyr, belongs to the latter category. Whereas all the other extant Acts of the Persian Martyrs have been published long ago, for the most part in volumes II and IV of Paul Bedjan's *Acta Martyrum et Sanctorum*, the *History of Ma'in* has never hitherto been published in full, and so it has been chosen as an appropriate text to inaugurate this new series of bilingual editions of the Persian Martyr Acts, whose aim is to make these interesting works more accessible to scholars and other readers.

I take the opportunity to thank Adam Becker, the General Editor of this new series, for his helpful comments, corrections and suggestions.

Sebastian Brock

ܕܘܒܪ̈ܢܐ ܕܣܗ̈ܕܐ ܦܪ̈ܣܝܐ

27th March, 2008

INTRODUCTION

INTRODUCTION AND OUTLINE

The *History of Ma'in* of Sinjar, a general under Shapur II (309–79) who converted to Christianity and suffered as a confessor, has hitherto been known only from the annotated German summary by Hoffmann and an article by Fiey.[1] The work falls into four main sections:

1–3. Introduction; his origins.
4–32. His conversion, instruction and baptism.
33–69. His sufferings at the hands of Shapur, and the intervention of a Roman ambassador.
70–91. His subsequent life, and death.

SYNOPSIS

1–2. The aim of the work is to give strength and encouragement to people through the example of virtuous men, in this case, Ma'in. As buildings need good foundations, so the narrative should start at the beginning of his life.
3. His origin and education.
4–5. Astonished by the endurance of the Christians he is persecuting, he asks himself, who is this Christ for whom they are suffering. In this way he is led by God to repentance.
6. An angel instructs Benjamin, an ascetic, to go to Sinjar, in readiness to instruct Ma'in.

---

[1] G. Hoffmann, *Auszüge aus syrischen Akten persischer Märtyrer* (Abhandlungen für die Kunde des Morgenlandes VII.3; Leipzig, 1880), 28–33 (cited as Hoffmann); J-M. Fiey, "Ma'in, général de Sapor II, confesseur et évêque," *Le Muséon* 84 (1971): 437–53 (cited as Fiey). Fiey subsequently provided a summary in his *Saints syriaques* (Princeton, NJ, 2004), in the entry for Ma'in (see also that for Benjamin). Reference was nevertheless made to the work (on the basis of Hoffmann's summary) by a number of scholars, notably Cumont and Musil (see notes to **6** and **71**).

7. The martyrdom of Doda, who is skinned alive, finally brings Ma'in to faith in Christ.
8. In a night vision he is told to go to the nearby mountain.
9–28. Benjamin receives him and proceeds to instruct him, providing a long catechism on the course of salvation history: Creation (**11–13**); the Exodus (**14–15**); how the Israelites worshipped Baal and killed the prophets (**16**); the sending of the Son: his mission on earth, ending with the Ascension (**17–27**); conclusion (**28**).
29–30. Benjamin, who had been ordained by Barse, bishop of Edessa, baptizes him.
31–32. Benjamin's farewell and instruction, warning him of what was to come.
33–34. Shapur looks for his general, and is told of his conversion.
35–36. A search party is sent out.
37–44. Ma'in is brought before Shapur, and a report is given of his interrogation by the shah.
45. Shapur orders that Ma'in be scourged; at the same time the *marzban* Walgash is sent off to search for Benjamin.
46–47. A Roman ambassador arrives, and sees Ma'in being scourged. On his return he reports this to Constantine.
48–51. In response, Constantine treats the Persian hostages at his court harshly; he writes to Shapur in threatening terms, and the young hostages also send letters to their parents. These letters are all taken back to Persia by the ambassador (henceforth called "the believing man").
52. Benjamin is found, and put to death.
53. Benjamin appears to Ma'in in the night, and foretells what is to come.
54–56. Shapur is delayed some 50 days from dealing with Ma'in due to war with the Greeks. Once he is able to do so, he sends for him and interrogates him.
57–58. Shapur orders that Ma'in be tortured, but while this is being carried out the ambassador turns up. On seeing Ma'in, he goes and kisses his feet, and then presents Constantine's letter to the trembling Shapur. He then makes specific demands of Shapur.
59. Shapur duly sends out orders that Christians should not be harmed, under pain of death.
60–61. He then gives instructions for Ma'in to be escorted to the palace to eat with him. Ma'in, however, refuses, but eventually agrees to eat with the ambassador food that has been brought from the West.
62–66. The ambassador invites Ma'in back to the Roman Empire, but he declines, saying that he has missionary work to do in Persia. He likewise

declines the services of a doctor, but gives the ambassador a message to pass on to Constantine. The ambassador begs for a relic from his clothes.
67–69. Before leaving, the ambassador demands written confirmation that Shapur and his nobles will not harm Ma'in. On his way back he is accompanied by Ma'in as far as Edessa. On hearing the account of all that happened, the emperor institutes a special commemoration for strangers.
70. Ma'in returns to Sinjar, sells his possessions, and starts out on a career of building monasteries—96 in all. He also makes provision for their liturgical services.
71–72. He converts and heals many people. In due course he travels to 'Anat, where he lives with a lion which he has tamed: it remains with him for 12 years, 7 of which are in his cell at 'Anat, and 5 where he was converted.
73–75. He comes upon a pagan festival being held in the vicinity of the village of Shadwa, near the town Agrippos, which king Agrippa had built on the Euphrates. He preaches to the people and converts many.
76. He vows to spend the rest of his life there, but on two occasions he is snatched away in the spirit.
77–79. He experiences torments from demons who re-enact the trauma of his earlier tortures, but he is encouraged to persevere by a voice from heaven.
80. The lion's habits are described: it only kills wild animals.
81–82. Ma'in suffers further attacks by demons.
83–91. Summary of his life: the healings he effects (**83**), the 96 monasteries he built on the mountain of Sinjar (**84**); how he sensed his end coming and gathered "the encampment" and prayed for them (**85–89**; his prayer is given); his death and burial (**89**), and a final summary of the chronology of his life (**90–91**).

LITERARY MODELS

The narrative has certain literary pretensions, thus setting it apart from most of the other martyrdoms said to have occurred under Shapur. These are manifested by the topos of the need "to lay the foundations" of the narrative (section **2**), and in particular by the various allusions to biblical figures: thus the description of Ma'in as "a valiant athlete" (**2**, *atliṭa ḥliṣa*) deliberately reflects the same phrase in IV Maccabees 6:10. The relationship of Benjamin to Ma'in reflects that of Ananias to Paul: Ma'in, like Paul, is "a chosen vessel" (**6** ~ Acts 9:16), and Benjamin, like Ananias, is told in a dream to go to instruct the newly converted Ma'in. Another resonance with Acts is provided by Ma'in's asking, after his long instruction, "what now hinders my baptism?", based on the Ethiopian eunuch's words to Philip (Acts 8:36). Several other, no doubt deliberate, reflections of biblical wording can be found throughout, quite apart from a fair number of direct biblical quotations (italicized in the English translation).

Links with other hagiographical narratives are harder to establish, though it is quite likely that the distinctive phrase in the opening paragraph, "the splendid and perfect manner of life" is derived from the *Life of Abraham of Qidun*, where it likewise appears at the beginning.[2] This particular combination of the two adjectives with *dubbare* is definitely unusual, and seems not to be found in other published Lives. Two further links with this Life can be found: Abraham quotes Psalm 118:12 against Satan, just as Ma'in quotes it against the demons (*Life of Abraham*, 15; *Ma'in*, **86**). And in the *Life of Abraham* specific mention of his *galla* and *kutina* is made; it is precisely the *kutina* of Ma'in for which the Roman ambassador asks (*Life of Abraham*, 4; *Ma'in*, **66**).

There are also a few general parallels to be found with the *Martyrdom of Qardagh*:[3] the role of the ascetic Benjamin, living in a cave, is not unlike that of 'Abdisho', who is Qardagh's mentor. Furthermore, both Ma'in and Qardagh at points of crisis quote Psalm 118:12 (*Ma'in*, **78**, *Qardagh*, 50)—though this also features in the *Life of Abraham of Qidun*, as noted above. Likewise, both men are encouraged by a heavenly voice (*Ma'in*, **79**, *Qardagh*, 44). It seems unlikely, however, that there is any direct literary contact (whichever way) here.

DATE OF COMPOSITION: THE LINGUISTIC EVIDENCE

There are no very clear indications in the language of the narrative to indicate an approximate date of composition. Two details, however, suggest a date not before the sixth century: in **4** the reflexive *naḥḥem hu leh* "he resurrected himself" occurs, and in **86** the construction *emar lwat* (rather than *emar l-*) is found. Although the use of *hu leh* as a reflexive is already occasionally found in Ephrem, it is much more characteristic of sixth- and seventh-century usage, and this is supported by the use of *lwat* with the verb *emar*, modelled on Greek *eipein pros* (alongside the dative): this is not found in texts earlier than the sixth century in the sense "to say to" (as opposed to

[2] T. J. Lamy, ed., *Sancti Ephraemi Syri Hymni et Sermones*, IV (Malines, 1902), cols 13–84.

[3] English translation in J. T. Walker, *The Legend of Mar Qardagh. Narrative and Christian Heroism in Late Antique Iraq* (Berkeley, 2006), 19–69.

"to say with reference to"). A date much later than the sixth century is unlikely, given the presence of the use of the "infinitive absolute" (**4**, **11**), which becomes very rare later, and the absence of any tell-tale later lexical items (such as *ṭubtana*, instead of *ṭubana*, which the author regularly uses). Likewise the choice of *bar kyana* (in **17**) to represent Greek *homoousios* conforms with older usage, in contrast to the sixth-century innovations such as *bar ituta* and *shawe b-usya*. A feature of terminology would also seem to point to (at least) the sixth century: in **32** the Roman Empire is referred to as "Romania": although the use of this term with this sense in Greek is first attested in Epiphanius in the late fourth century, it does not seem to become more widely found until the sixth century.[4] The evidence of the use of the Persian term *marzbana*, "marzban" is less clear: elsewhere in the acts of martyrs under Shapur it only occurs in the *Martyrdom of Qardag*,[5] which is definitely a sixth-century work. It does, however, feature earlier in the acts of Narsai,[6] a martyr under Yazdgard I (399–420), whose acts were probably the work of a certain Abgar, writing shortly after the martyrdom.[7] In the *Acts of Pethion*, a martyr under Yazdgard II (439–57), mention is made of a marzban of Adhorbaigan (*AMS* II, 620). This linguistic evidence, slight though it may be, happens to fit well with Fiey's dating of the work (on which, see below under *Historicity*).

That the author was writing within the Roman Empire is self-evident. This is clearly implied, for example, by **89** where mention is made of "two of *our* brethren", to whom Ma'in hands over authority before his death, which takes place in Roman territory. See also the annotation to **55** and **77**.

FIEY'S DATING OF THE *HISTORY*

In his study of the *History* Fiey gives a *terminus post quem* of c. 508 for its composition (p. 450). This date is entirely dependant on his proposal that

---

[4] See J. Irmscher, "Sulle origini del concetto Romania," in *Popoli e Spazio Romano tra diritto e profezia* (Da Roma alla Terza Roma: Studi, 3; Naples, 1983 [1986]), 421–9. It had its origin in popular usage (thus it features in acclamations in the early seventh-century *Chronicon Paschale*, ed. L. Dindorf [Berlin, 1832], 610, 622). For some other Syriac attestations, see the annotation to **32.**

[5] E.g. sections **5**, **48**. For the sigillographic evidence of the term, see Ph. Gignoux, "L'organisation administrative sasanide: le cas du marzban," *Jerusalem Studies in Arabic and Islam* 4 (1984): 1–29.

[6] *AMS* IV, 175 (of Beth Aramaye), 207 (present in Nisibis).

[7] See P. Devos, "Abgar: hagiographe perse méconnu (début du Ve siècle)," *Analecta Bollandiana* 83 (1965): 303–28.

Dura (**5**) should be taken as a corruption of Dara, which was only founded by Anastasius c. 508; this, however, is totally implausible seeing that Dura is specifically described as being "ruined", which of course rules out Dara, but fits Dura Europos very well. Though the basis for his *terminus post quem* falls away, it has been seen above that, on the evidence of the language, a sixth-century date seems in any case likely, on other grounds. Fiey is more plausible in his suggestion that the *History* was written at a monastery that had grown up on the site of Mar Ma'in's cell at Shadba (=Shadwa, Shadbo), 6 miles from Europos, and on the basis of this he is able to give c. 636, the end of Byzantine rule in that area, as the *terminus ante quem*, since the author is clearly writing at a time when the Byzantine emperor controlled the area.

TOPOGRAPHY

Ma'in himself is said to have been from Sinjar (**3**); since this is specifically said to be "in Persian territory" a date after 363 is implied. It was in Sinjar that he was converted by Benjamin, who went there from Dura (evidently Dura Europos; **6**). It is not stated where Shapur was when he sent for Ma'in (**33**) and subsequently subjected him to torture. When Ma'in is eventually released, thanks to the Roman envoy, he travels with the envoy as far as Edessa, but then returns to Sinjar (**70**), where he began his program of monastic building. He then goes to 'Anat ('Ana; **71**), on the Euphrates,[8] and after some years he proceeds north westwards up the Euphrates to a village named Shadwa (later, Shadbo, **91**), said to be some six miles from "Agrippos" ('GRPWS; **73**), which is evidently a corruption of 'WRPWS, Europos,[9] quite a long distance further up the Euphrates. Europos corresponds to the modern Jerabis/Gerablus. Shadwa is described variously as a *castra* (**75**), suggesting it had once been a Roman military outpost, and as an "encampment" (**86**), whose inhabitants were probably Arabs. It was there that he died, and a passing mention of "*our* brethren" (**89**) indicates that the author of the Life would have belonged to a monastic community that had grown up on the same site.

---

[8] A Syrian Orthodox bishopric is attested at 'Ana from the 7th to the 10th century: J-M. Fiey, *Pour un Oriens Christianus Novus* (Beirut, 1993), 164–5 and (in more detail) in *Parole de l'Orient* 5 (1974): 362–8. 'Ana was a centre for the Taghlabite Arabs.

[9] See the annotation to **73**.

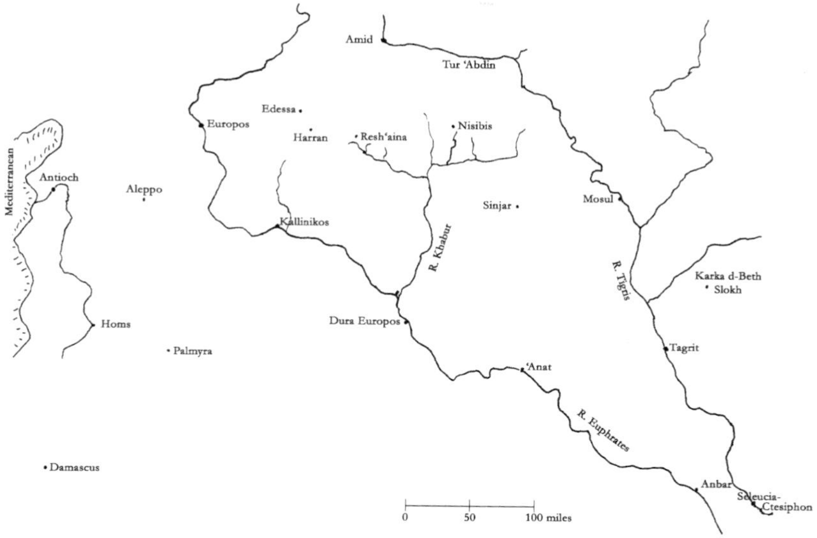

Fig. 1 Broader Mesopotamian region relevant to the *History of Mar Ma'in*

THE CHRONOLOGICAL DATA

The final sections (**90–91**) provide a chronological summary of Ma'in's life: he was converted to Christianity at the age of 60, in the first year of Constantine's reign. He then spent three years in prison, eventually to be released thanks to the intervention of a Roman envoy. The next thirty seven years were spent in building activities in the Sinjar region, followed by seven years in a cell near 'Anat, and then six years in the village Shadbo, where he died at the age of 114 (this more or less corresponds to the sum of 60+3+37+7+6). Earlier in the narrative, he is said to have been baptized by Benjamin who had been ordained by Barse, bishop of Edessa (**30**); and subsequently it is stated that the same Barse later made Ma'in a bishop (**68**). The arrival of a Roman envoy on two successive occasions is mentioned in **46** and **57**, and in **54** we are told that in the intervening period, for about fifty days, Shapur was diverted from judging the case of Ma'in due to incursions by "Greeks" (*yawnaye*). On his second visit the Roman envoy conveys a threatening letter from Constantine, addressed to Shapur. In **45** we are also provided with a name (Walgash) for the Marzban who was sent to kill Ma'in's teacher, the hermit Benjamin.

HISTORICITY

It will be obvious at once that this chronological information in the *History* poses serious problems. The Emperor Constantine died in 337, but the outbreak of Shapur's persecutions only took place several years later, very probably in 344.[10] To make matters worse, a synchronism is given between Ma'in's conversion, at the age of c. 60, and the first year of Constantine. Confusion between Constantine and Constantius (II, 337–362), easy in Syriac script, might have helped to resolve this,[11] but the references to Barse, bishop of Edessa, rule that out as a solution, since he was bishop in Edessa from 361 to 373, when he was deposed by Valens (Barse's death in

[10] The date has long been disputed, thanks to the conflicting evidence for the date of Simeon bar Sabba'e's martyrdom: arguments in favour of 341 have been made, but 344 now seems most likely (see R. W. Burgess, "The dates of the Martyrdom of Simeon bar Sabba'e and the Great Massacre," *Analecta Bollandiana* 117 (1999): 9–45).

[11] The situation late in the reign of Constantius II might have provided a suitable background; for this see, R. C. Blockley, "Constantius II and Persia," in *Studies in Latin Literature and Roman History*, ed., C. Deroux (Collection Latomus 206; Bruxelles, 1989), 465–90.

March 378 is recorded in the *Chronicle of Edessa*). It is evident, then, that the author had no clear conception of the chronology of events in the fourth century. This, in fact, is not too surprising if, as seems likely, the text belongs to about the sixth century. The author has, however, taken care to make the figures given for the chronology of Ma'in's own life consistent in his summary in **90–91**.

In his study of the *History* Fiey has offered a plausible explanation of how the conflicting synchronisms have come about. According to him, the one synchronism which is likely to be genuine is that with bishop Barse. Since the emperor for most of the time of Barse's episcopate was the "Arian" Valens (364–78), it was clearly preferable to have a more suitable emperor on the throne, and who better than Constantine himself? Using Barse as the one reliable chronological anchor, Fiey then goes on to suggest that the three years during which Ma'in was in prison (**90**), as well as the "fifty days" when war with "the Greeks" diverted Shapur's attention from Ma'in's case (**54**), should be seen as corresponding to the time of fighting over Armenia during the period 370–373. This would at least seem a reasonable possibility.[12] It should be noted, however, that it assumes retaining the manuscript's somewhat problematic reading *ywny'* at **54**, and rejecting Hoffmann's suggestion that this is a corruption of *kywny'*, <*Ch*>*ionaye*, Chionites (i.e. Huns);[13] however, even with Hoffmann's conjecture, the episode involved might fit movements of the Huns slightly later in the 370s.

Fiey concludes his article by offering the following chronology for Ma'in's life, using the figures given in the text and attaching them to an absolute chronology based on the points mentioned:

Born c. 310
Conversion c. 370
Death of Benjamin c. 371/2
Ma'in's release from prison, end of the summer 373, after the armistice with Valens, followed by a visit to Edessa where Barse makes him a bishop.
Building activities in Sinjar c. 374–410
Move to 'Anat/'Ana c. 411

---

[12] For the situation between the Romans and Persians over Armenia at this time, see R. C. Blockley, "The division of Armenia between the Romans and the Persians at the end of the fourth century AD," *Historia* 36 (1987): 222–34, especially 227–8.

[13] See further the annotation to **54**.

Move to Shadba, near Europos c. 418
Dies aged 114 c. 424

As Fiey points out, many of the figures given in the *History* are not likely to be reliable, but he suggests that the nucleus of c. 370–374 does seem reasonably assured.

THE MANUSCRIPT

The sole manuscript to transmit the *History of Ma'in* is British Library Add. 12,174, a large hagiographical manuscript, dated Teshri I, 1508 of the Seleucid era (= October AD 1196), containing 71 lives.[14] It was written in the famous Monastery of Mar Barsaumo, near Malatya, the residence of the patriarch in that period. Of particular interest at the end of the manuscript is a note by Patriarch Michael the Great, stating that it had been commissioned by the deacon Saliba especially for the library (*biblotiqi* = Greek *bibliotheke*) of the monastery to fill a gap in its holdings. This was part of the gradual work of replenishing the library after the disastrous fire of July 30, 1183.[15]

The *History of Ma'in* features on ff. 388v-395r and is numbered 67. It comes as the last of a short series of Persian martyrs: the Martyrs of Tur Ber'ain, Simeon bar Sabba'e, Pusai, Martha, Shahdost, Tarbo, 120 Martyrs, and Pethion. All these, with the exception of Pethion, were martyrs in the reign of Shapur II. The *History* is also given a secondary number, "19," which refers to the sub-series of Martyrdoms. A similar organisation of the contents is to be found in the more or less contemporary pair of hagiographical manuscripts, Damascus Patriarchate 12/17 and 12/18;[16] indeed, it is very possible that the collection of lives in Add. 12,174 was specifically assembled in order to complement the contents of the two Damascus manuscripts.

---

[14] W. Wright, *Catalogue of the Syriac Manuscripts in the British Museum acquired since the year 1838* (London, 1872), III, 1123–39.

[15] Described by Michael in his Chronicle XXI.2 (ed. J-B. Chabot, *Chronique de Michel le Syrien* (repr. Bruxelles, 1963), III, pp. 391–2 = IV, pp. 726–7). Cf. E. Honigmann, *Le Couvent de Barsauma et le Patriarcat Jacobite d'Antioche et de Syrie* (CSCO Subs. 7, 1954), 48. For other autograph notes by Patriarch Michael, see F. Nau, "Sur quelques autographes de Michel le Syrien," *Revue de l'Orient Chrétien* II.9 (1914): 378–97.

[16] A list of the contents can be found in *Parole de l'Orient* 19 (1994): 608–14.

THE PRESENT EDITION

The text below reproduces that in the manuscript with the following exceptions:

- section numbers have been supplied;
- abbreviations have been tacitly resolved;
- obvious scribal errors have been corrected; these concern the following:
  (a) omission of *waw* in the 3rd masc. plural of perfects; thus the manuscript has:
  (**14**) ܘܫܥܒܕ...ܘܚܣܢܬ, (**16**) ܫܕܪ, (**57**) ܕܐܬܐܠܨ, and (**73**) ܕܢܚܠ ܘܢܒ.
  (b) omission of a letter through haplography; thus the manuscript has:
  (**4**) ܐܠܗܘܢ, (**90**) ܘܐܪܒܬܥܣܪ̈ܐ.
- some combinations written together in the manuscript have been separated; thus the manuscript has: (**31**) ܡܛܠܗܢܐ, (**36 63**) ܘܟܠܗܕܐ, (**76**) ܟܠܗܝ, and (**28**) ܡܢܘܕܡ.
- *syame* have been added to ܡܢܐ (the absence of *syame* from ܡܢܐ is in fact found in a number of medieval manuscripts).
- some unusual spellings have been standardized: thus in **20** the manuscript has ܕܐܠܗ, in **23** it has ܫܪ̈ܬ, and in **66** it has ܬܣܒܝ .

All other deviations from the manuscript are indicated in the apparatus.

APPARATUS

The reading of the manuscript is given to the right of the square bracket.

1 ܡܕܝܢܐ] ܡܕܝܢܬܐ

4 ܐܠܗܗܘܢ] ܐܠܗܘܢ

6 ܕܡܐܢܐ] ܡܐܢܐ

14 ܘܡܟܒܒܪ̈ܘܬܐ] ܘܡܟܒܪ̈ܘܬܐ

18 ܒܕ] ܟܕ

42 ܕܬܫܬܪܐ] ܕܬܫܪܐ

48 ܗܘܘ] ܗܘܐ

49 ܘܠܢ] ܘܠܐ

56 ܛܒ̈ܐܬܐ] ܛܒ̈ܬܐ

63 ܐܠܐ ܡܢܐ ܕܬܠܡܝܕܬ] ܐܠܐ ܕܬܠܡܝܕ

66 ܕܠܒܫ] ܕܠܒܫܐ

73 ܗܘܬ] ܗܘܐ

77 ܗܘ̈ܝ] ܗܘܐ

77 ܡܪ̈ܕܐ] ܡܪ̈ܪܐ
For possible corrections that may also be required to the text, see annotation to **32** and **54**.

TEXT AND TRANSLATION

The History of the Holy Mar Ma'in, from Sinjar, a town in Persian territory

1. The splendid and perfect manner of life of those virtuous men who are rich in God but poor in transitory possessions, fighters against error and warriors against the Adversary, friends of God and enemies of Satan, everywhere and in every town, has been fully described in writing to give strength to the hesitance of weak minds, so that people might be confirmed in the truth of the Gospel of the glory of Jesus Christ, the Son of God. These matters were not written down out of pride or vain glory, but to the glory and praise of these elect and upright men who acted valiantly, as well as of God, in that they are to be found everywhere.

2. We shall now recount and relate before all of you who love God the splendid and perfect manner of life of this valiant man, the mighty athlete Mar Ma'in, telling how he turned from error to knowledge of the truth, abandoning the error of the Accuser and drawing near to Christ. Just as a wise architect, on commencing a building, first lays firm foundations, and only then builds and completes his edifice (cf. Luke 6:48, 14:29), so we too should start our narrative with the beginning of the blessed man's life.

3. This blessed Mar Ma'in, then, was from the town of Sinjar in Persian territory. He was very well educated in literature and in the Magian religion; he was extremely clever and was proficient and skilled at everything. As a result of his intellectual attainments he won the favour of king Shapur, who appointed him a general.

4. When the martyrs of Christ were being put to death he saw how they endured terrible sufferings and afflictions for Christ's sake, refusing to deny him. He said to himself, "Who is this Christ, the so-called Nazarene (Matt 2:23 etc.), whom these people confess in front of everyone, each one of them crying out without any inhibition, 'We are dying for the sake of Christ who was crucified. Just as he died for our sakes, so let us too die for his sake'? And I perceive that he actually helps them in all afflictions. I am amazed, too, at two words uttered from their mouths, truly astonishing and hard for people to accept: on the one hand they say that he is a man, and confess that he was actually crucified, that he died and was buried, and then arose and resuscitated himself; on the other hand, they also say that he is God, and Son of God; that he as-

Add.12,174, ff.388v-395r

ܬܘܒ ܬܫܥܝܬܐ ܕܩܕܝܫܐ ܡܪܝ ܡܥܝܢ ܕܐܬܘܗܝ ܡܢ ܫܝܓܪ
ܡܕܝܢܬܐ ܕܒܝܬ ܦܪ̈ܣܝܐ

1. ܕܘܒܪܐ ܫܦܝܪܐ ܘܡܫܬܒܚܢܐ ܕܐܢܫ̈ܐ ܬܩܝܢܐ ܒܬܪܗ ܒܐܠܗܐ. ܘܡܗܦܟܢܐ ܕܡܢ ܡܫܝܚܐ ܒܒܘܪ̈ܐ ܡ̈ܬܚܬܝܐ ܕܠܗܘܒ ܛܘܒܢ. ܣܠܩܬܐ ܕܠܗܘܒ ܒܠܒܪܐ. ܕܢܚܐ ܕܐܠܗܐ ܘܒܠܒ̈ܒܐ ܕܗܘܢܐ. ܒܟܠ ܐܬܪ ܘܒܟܠ ܡܕܝܢܐ. ܐܬܟܬܒ ܘܐܬܬܢܝܚ ܠܬܘܪܪܐ ܕܩܠܝܛܘܬ ܪܚܝܐ ܪܕܦܐ ܕܡܬܪܪܘܢ ܒܥܪܘܗ ܕܐܘܠܝܨܘܢ. ܕܫܘܒܚܗ ܕܫܘܒ ܡܫܝܚܐ ܒܪܗ ܕܐܠܗܐ. ܠܗ ܒܥܪ ܠܫܘܒܗܪܐ ܘܠܫܘܒܚܐ ܣܝܡܐ ܐܬܟܬܒܘ: ܐܠܐ ܠܫܘܒܚܐ ܘܠܬܘܠܫܬܐ ܕܠܗܘܢ ܕܒ̈ܢܝܐ ܒ̈ܢܝܢܐ ܕܒܝܬܐ. ܘܕܐܠܗܐ ܕܒܟܠܐ ܐܢܘܢ ܒܟܠ ܐܬܪ܀

2. ܕܢܫܬܥܐ ܕܝܢ ܗܫܐ ܘܢܬܢܐ ܡܕܡܝܢܘܢ ܕܒܠ ܥܘܕܪܗ ܐܠܗܐ ܒܠ ܕܘܒܪܐ ܫܦܝܪܐ ܘܡܫܬܒܚܢܐ ܕܗܢܐ ܓܒܪܐ ܣܠܩܬܐ: ܐܬܠܛܦ ܣܠܝܩܐ ܡܪܝ ܡܥܝܢ. ܕܐܬܒܥܐ ܡܢ ܛܘܒܢܘܬܐ ܠܡܕܒܪܬܐ ܕܫܪܪܐ ܦܢܐ. ܘܠܘܬ ܡܫܝܚܐ ܡܢ ܛܘܒܢܘܬܗ ܕܐܒܠܗܪ̈ܝܐ ܐܬܦܢܝ. ܘܐܟܡܢ ܐܪܕܟܠܐ ܚܟܝܡܐ ܕܒܢܐ ܕܡܫܪܐ ܒܒܝܬܐ ܠܗܘܕܡ ܫܬܐܣܘܬܐ ܣܐܡ ܘܡܫܪܪ: ܘܗܘܕܡ ܒܢܐ ܘܡܫܟܠܠ ܒܝܬܗ: ܗܟܢܐ ܐܦ ܚܢܢ ܙܕܩ ܠܢ. ܕܡܢ ܫܘܪܝܐ ܕܕܘܒܪܗ ܕܛܘܒܢܐ ܢܫܬܥܐ ܬܫܥܝܬܐ܀

3. ܗܢܐ ܗܟܝܠ ܛܘܒܢܐ ܡܪܝ ܡܥܝܢ: ܐܬܘܗܝ ܗܘܐ ܡܢ ܫܝܓܪ ܡܕܝܢܬܐ ܕܒܝܬ ܦܪ̈ܣܝܐ. ܘܗܟܢ ܐܬܪܗ ܒܗܦܪܐ ܘܒܡܟܬܫܘܬܐ. ܘܗܟܢ ܚܟܝܡ ܗܘܐ ܘܕܪܝܐ ܘܡܗܝܪ ܒܟܠܡܕܡ. ܘܡܛܠ ܚܟܡܬܗ ܘܫܘܟܠܗ ܫܦܪ ܠܥܝܢܝ ܡܠܟܐ: ܘܥܒܕܗ ܠܗ ܪܒ ܚܝܠܐ܀

4. ܘܒܪ ܡܬܩܛܠܝܢ ܗܘܘ ܣܗܕ̈ܘܗܝ ܕܡܫܝܚܐ. ܚܙܐ ܗܘܐ ܕܐܝܟܢܐ ܣܒܠܝܢ ܗܘܘ ܣܓ̈ܝܐܐ ܒܢ̈ܫܐ ܘܐܘܠܨ̈ܢܐ ܡܛܠ ܡܫܝܚܐ: ܘܠܐ ܟܦܪܝܢ ܗܘܘ. ܘܐܡܪ ܗܘܐ ܗܘ ܒܢܦܫܗ. ܡܢܘ ܒܗ ܗܢܐ ܡܫܝܚܐ ܕܚܝܠܐ ܡܬܟܢܐ. ܘܗܠܝܢ ܡܟܪܝܢ ܘܐܡܪܝܢ ܡܕܡ ܒܠܥ. ܘܗܟܝܢ ܕܠܐ ܒܗܘܕܐ ܒܠܚܘܕ ܡܢܗܘܢ. ܕܡܛܠ ܡܫܝܚܐ ܕܐܬܛܠܒ ܡܬܚܢܢܝܢ. ܐܡܪܐ ܕܗܘ ܡܛܠ ܣܠܝܩܝܢ: ܐܦ ܚܢ ܢܗܘܬ ܣܠܝܩܘܗܝ, ܘܗܘܐ ܚܙܐ ܐܢܐ ܕܡܕܪܘ ܡܟܪ ܠܗܘܢ ܒܟܠ

cended to his Father and sits at his right hand, and that he will come again in glory at the end of time to judge the living and the dead. I am truly amazed and astonished at all this, that they call him both man and God, dead and resuscitator. I have no idea what to say about this: if he is a man, then why do they die for his sake, for there is no mortal on earth in my opinion who is able to be struck on the cheek (cf. Matt 5:39) for his friend's sake. But maybe he is in truth a god, and it is for that reason that they endure affliction, refusing to deny him even to the point of death. Perhaps he has some other kind of wealth, better than ours, to give them, seeing that, even though we cajole them with wealth, presents and huge gifts, pressing them with harsh threats, fetters, imprisonment and bitter forms of death, they show no desire for gifts, no love for wealth; they do not want any presents, and they are not afraid of the sword or fearful of the fire; they are not moved by threats, they think nothing of the world and all that is in it; instead their eyes are fixed on heaven where they say their Lord is. What to make of all this I have no idea. What does their god want? And if he is the true God and wants me, having made known and showed himself to me, then I too should have believed in him like them."

5. Then, in his grace, God who is at all times concerned for the recovery of sinners, enticing them to repentance by all sorts of means, showed his concern for this errant man as well, so that he might straightaway turn him towards himself, away from error.

6. In a deserted town called Dura there happened to be a blessed man, a "mourner" called Benjamin, a wonderful and godly person. As he was standing in prayer in a cave he saw an angel of God in front of him who

ܐܘܠܨ̈ܢܝܢ. ܘܡܬܕܪܫܢ ܐܢܐ ܕܡܢ ܦܘܩܕܢܗܘܢ ܬܬܪ̈ܝܢ ܩ̈ܠܝܢ
ܐܡܪܝܢ ܘܠܟ ܬܡܪܗܘܢ: ܘܚܫܩܝܢ ܠܡܫܡܫܘܬܐ ܕܫ̈ܐܕܐ. ܐܡܪܝܢ
ܓܒܪ ܕܫ̈ܐܕܐ ܗܘ. ܘܡܫܬܕܪ ܒܗ ܕܡܢ ܦܠܓܗ ܐܢ ܦܠܓ. ܘܡܫܬ
ܘܐܬܦܩܕ: ܘܦܩܕ ܘܫܡܥ ܗܘ ܠܗ܀ ܘܐܡܪܝܢ ܬܘܒ ܕܐܠܗܐ ܗܘ
ܘܒܪ ܐܠܗܐ. ܘܫܠܡ ܠܘܬ ܐܒܘܗܝ. ܘܠܐ ܡܢ ܡܚܝܢܘ. ܘܬܘܒ
ܐܬܬܐ ܒܥܘܒܥܐ ܠܣܪܬܐ ܕܪܕܘܢ ܫܢܐ ܘܡܥܠܬܐ. ܘܒܗܠܝܢ ܦܠܓ
ܬܚܝܘܗܝ ܐܢܐ ܘܡܬܕܪܫ ܐܢܐ. ܕܦܘܩ ܠܗ ܒܪܫܐ ܘܐܠܗܐ.
ܡܠܬܐ ܘܡܫܝܚܝܐ. ܘܡܢܐ ܐܡܪ ܥܠ ܗܠܝܢ ܠܐ ܝܕܥ ܐܢܐ.
ܕܐܢ ܒܪܫܐ ܗܘ. ܠܡܢܐ ܡܦܠܬܢ ܣܓܕܘܗܝ. ܠܐ ܓܒܪ ܐܢܬ
ܒܪܫܐ ܥܠ ܐܪܥܐ ܐܝܟ ܕܒܪܚܡܝ ܕܝܠܝ ܕܡܫܡܫ ܕܢܒܠܥ ܦܓܪܐ
ܣܠܩ ܙܩܝܦܗ. ܐܠܐ ܒܪܐ ܒܙܪܪܐ ܐܠܗܐ ܗܘ: ܘܡܬܠܠ ܗܢܐ
ܡܬܐܠܝܨ ܕܠܐ ܢܒܦܘܩܢ ܒܗ ܒܕܡܐ ܠܡܘܬܐ. ܕܒܒܪ
ܒܡܘܬܐ ܐܣܝܪܐ ܐܝܬ ܠܗ ܕܢܬܠ ܠܗܘܢ ܕܡܫܬܪ ܡܢ ܗܢܐ
ܕܝܠܝ. ܗܐ ܓܒܪ ܒܡܘܬܐ ܘܐܦ ܒܡ̈ܗܝܡܢܘܬܐ ܘܒܕ̈ܚܠܬܐ
ܪ̈ܘܪܒܐ ܡܫܪܝܢ ܠܗܘܢ. ܘܒܠܘܩܒܠܗܘܢ ܡ̈ܠܐ ܘܒܐܣܘܪ̈ܐ
ܘܒܣܒ̈ܠܬܐ ܘܡܫ̈ܘܬܐ ܡܪ̈ܝܪܐ ܐܠܝܨܝܢ ܠܗܘܢ. ܘܠܐ
ܠܡܗ̈ܘܡܬܐ ܪ̈ܓܝܢ ܘܐܦܠܐ ܠܡܘܬܐ ܙܒܝܢ. ܘܠܐ ܒܕ̈ܝܢܐ
ܝܩܝܪ. ܘܠܐ ܡܢ ܗܦܟܐ ܙܢܝܢ. ܘܠܐ ܡܢ ܢܘܪܐ ܕܠܝܩ. ܘܠܐ
ܡܢ ܠܘܫ̈ܒܐ ܡܬܬܙܝܥܝܢ. ܘܠܐ ܚܠܒܐ ܘܒܠ ܕܒܗ ܣܥܝܪ
ܠܗܘܢ. ܐܠܐ ܒܢ̈ܝܫܘܗܝ ܠܫܡܝܐ ܬܠܝܢ: ܘܐܡܪܝܢ ܕܬܡܢ ܗܘ
ܡܪܗܘܢ. ܘܡܢܐ ܐܡܪ ܥܠ ܗܠܝܢ ܠܐ ܝܕܥ ܐܢܐ. ܡܢ ܕܝܢ
ܝܕܥ ܐܠܗܘܗܝ ܘܐܢ ܐܠܗܐ ܗܘ ܕܒܙܪܪܐ ܘܢܩܦ ܠܗ ܒܗ:
ܘܐܘܕܒ ܘܫܘ ܠܝ ܢܦܫܗ: ܘܐܦ ܐܢܐ ܡܗܝܡܢ ܗܘܝܬ ܒܗ
ܐܒܘܬܗܘܢ܀

5. ܘܗܕܝܢ ܐܠܗܐ ܒܛܝܒܘܬܗ: ܗܘ ܕܒܟܠܢ ܒܥܐ ܠܗ ܥܠ
ܚܫܝܫܘܬܐ ܕܪ̈ܘܚܐ: ܘܡܚܪܝ ܠܗܘܢ ܒܟܠܙܒܢ ܠܡܬܒܘܬܐ:
ܐܦ ܥܠ ܗܢܐ ܛܘܒܢܐ ܐܬܚܫܒ ܠܗ ܕܒܚܝܠ ܢܦܫܗ ܠܬܘܒ
ܡܢ ܛܘܒܬܐ܀

6. ܐܝܬ ܗܘܐ ܒܡܕܝܢܬܐ ܚܕܐ ܚܪܒܬܐ ܕܡܬܩܪܝܐ ܕܘܪܐ.
ܒܪܢܫ ܚܕ ܛܘܒܢܐ ܐܒܝܠܐ: ܕܫܡܗ ܗܘܐ ܒܢܝܡܝܢ. ܒܪܢܫ
ܕܬܕܡܪܬܐ ܘܐܠܗܝܐ. ܗܢܐ ܒܪ ܩܝܡ ܘܚܝܠܐ ܒܡܥܒܕܬܐ:
ܚܕ ܗܘܐ ܠܟܠܗܝܢ ܕܐܠܗܐ ܒܪ ܩܝܡ ܩܕܡܘܗܝ. ܘܐܡܪ

said, "Be up and off to the mountain of Sinjar in the east; I am going to send king Shapur's general to you: show him the way of God, for he is one of God's chosen vessels" (cf. Acts 9:16).

7. At that time the blessed Doda died, skinned alive by king Shapur. It was he whom Mar Ma'in saw, and as a result came to faith in God.

8. The moment the blessed Benjamin heard this from the angel, without any doubt in his mind he started off at once in great eagerness, journeying through the desert until he came to the mountain of Sinjar, the place the angel had told him of. There he went into a cave, where he was praying for three days.

9. Then on the night of the third day, as Mar Ma'in was lying on his bed there appeared to him a wondrous man, his face illumined and glorious like the sun: no human tongue could describe his glory. He called out to him and said, "Be of good courage, Ma'in; arise, and ascend the mountain adjoining this town, and there you shall be told all that you are asking of Christ."

10. The next morning the blessed Mar Ma'in got up and set off for the place to which he had been told to go up. He made straight for the cave where the glorious Benjamin was. On entering it and catching sight of him he was afraid and frightened: "This man is an angel of God," he said; whereupon he fell on his face before him. Benjamin, however, told him, "Get up; you are the holy Mar Ma'in. The Lord God of heaven has sent me to you to teach you his mysteries and to strengthen you in faith in him. I am also to disclose him to you so that you may come to know him, just as you have requested of him. I shall give you his baptismal mark of salvation and establish you in his truth. So incline your heart towards me and listen to what I have to say about why the martyrs are dying for his sake, concerning this hope in which they are enduring all sorts of sufferings and afflictions in this world.

11. "God, along with the Child who issues from him, and his holy angels, wanting in his good will to establish a place of residence for the human race to live in, made heaven and earth (Gen 1:1), the sea and the dry land (Gen 1:10–11), the sun, the moon and the stars (Gen 1:16), light

ܠܗ. ܘܩܡ ܐܙܠ ܠܛܘܪܐ ܕܫܝܓܪ ܕܐܝܬ ܒܡܕܢܚܐ. ܘܗܘܐ ܠܒܪ
ܚܠܦ ܕܫܒܘܪ ܡܠܟܐ ܡܫܕܪ ܐܢܫ ܠܘܬܟ. ܫܡܥܗ̇ ܐܘܪܚܗ
ܕܐܠܗܐ: ܡܛܠ ܕܡܐܢܐ ܗܘ ܓܒܝܐ ܕܐܠܗܐ܀

7. ܒܗ ܕܝܢ ܒܝܘܡܐ ܗܘ̇ ܡܛܬ ܐܓܪܬܐ ܕܗܘܕܐ ܕܫܠܛܢܗ ܫܒܘܪ
ܡܠܟܐ. ܘܠܗ ܗܘ ܚܙܐ ܗܘܐ ܡܪܝ ܡܥܝܢ. ܘܐܦ ܡܛܠܬܗ
ܗܝܡܢ ܒܐܠܗܐ܀

8. ܛܘܒܢܐ ܕܝܢ ܒܫܡܝܢ ܡܢ ܕܫܡܥ ܡܢ ܡܠܐܟܐ ܗܠܝܢ. ܠܐ
ܐܬܦܠܓ ܐܠܐ ܩܡ ܡܫܕܪܐ ܒܫܦܝܘܬܐ ܩܕܝܫܬܐ. ܘܪܕܐ
ܒܗܘܪܟܐ ܘܐܬܐ ܠܛܘܪܐ ܕܫܝܓܪ ܠܐܝܟܐ ܕܐܡܪ ܠܗ
ܡܠܐܟܐ. ܘܥܠ ܠܬܡܢ ܠܡܥܪܬܐ. ܘܗܘܐ ܡܨܠܐ ܬܡܢ ܬܠܬܐ
ܝܘܡ̈ܝܢ܀

9. ܗܝܕܝܢ ܒܠܠܝܐ ܗܘ̇ ܕܬܠܬܐ: ܐܬܚܙܝ, ܠܗ ܠܡܪܝ ܡܥܝܢ ܒܪ ܡܓܘܫ
ܒܚܙܘܗ: ܓܒܪܐ ܚܕ ܬܡܝܗܐ. ܕܢܘܗܪ ܗܘܐ ܦܪܨܘܦܗ ܐܝܟ
ܫܡܫܐ ܘܫܒܝܚ ܗܘܐ. ܘܦܘܡܐ ܕܒܢ̈ܝܢܫܐ ܕܢܡܠܠ ܥܠ ܫܘܒܚܗ
ܠܐ ܡܨܐ ܗܘܐ. ܘܩܪܝܗ, ܘܐܡܪ ܠܗ. ܐܬܚܝܠ ܡܥܝܢ ܩܘܡ
ܦܘܩ ܠܛܘܪܐ ܕܡܕܢܚܬܐ ܗܕܐ: ܘܬܡܢ ܢܬܡܠܠ ܠܟ ܥܠ ܟܠ
ܕܒܥܐ ܐܢܬ ܡܢ ܡܫܝܚܐ܀

10. ܘܩܡ ܛܘܒܢܐ ܡܪܝ ܡܥܝܢ ܒܨܦܪܐ ܘܐܙܠ ܠܐܝܟܐ ܕܐܬܡܠܠ
ܥܡܗ ܕܢܫܐ. ܘܦܫܝܛܐܝܬ ܬܪܨ ܘܥܠ ܠܗ̇ ܡܥܪܬܐ ܕܐܬܘܗܝ,
ܗܘܐ ܒܗ̇ ܢܘܗܪܐ ܒܫܡܝܢ. ܘܟܕ ܥܠ ܘܣܓܕܗ, ܕܚܠ ܘܪܥܠ
ܘܐܡܪ. ܗܢܐ ܓܒܪܐ ܡܠܐܟܗ ܗܘ ܕܐܠܗܐ. ܘܢܦܠ ܥܠ
ܐܦ̈ܘܗܝ, ܘܣܓܕܗ. ܗܘ ܕܝܢ ܒܫܡܝܢ ܐܡܪ ܠܗ. ܩܘܡ ܠܟ. ܐܢܬ
ܗܘ ܡܕܝܢܐ ܡܪܝ ܡܥܝܢ. ܡܪܝܐ ܐܠܗܐ ܕܫܡܝܐ ܫܕܪܢ ܠܘܬܟ:
ܕܐܠܦܟ ܐܘܪ̈ܚܬܗ, ܘܐܫܪܪܟ ܒܗܝܡܢܘܬܗ. ܘܐܦ ܕܐ ܕܓܠܐ
ܠܟ ܥܠܘܗܝ, ܕܬܕܒܪܝܘܗܝ, ܐܝܟܢܐ ܕܫܐܠܬ ܡܢܗ. ܘܐܬܠ ܠܟ
ܪܘܫܡܗ ܕܨܠܝܒܐ: ܘܐܬܡܢܟ ܒܙܪܙܗ. ܕܒܗܠܝܢ ܡܢܐ ܡܢܬܗ
ܫܠܡܘܗܝ, ܡܫܕܪܐ ܘܥܠ ܐܢܫܐ ܡܕܢܚܐ ܥܠ ܚܝ̈ܝܢ ܡܫܝܚܝܝܢ
ܘܐܘܠܦܢܐ ܒܥܠܡܐ ܗܢܐ. ܟܠ ܗܫܐ ܠܘܬܝ, ܠܒܝ ܘܫܡܥ
ܡ̈ܠܝ܀

11. ܐܠܗܐ ܗܘ ܘܡܠܕܐ ܕܒܢܝܗ. ܘܡܠܐ̈ܟܘܗܝ, ܩܕ̈ܝܫܐ. ܘܒܪ ܝܕܥܐ
ܟܢܫܘܗܝ ܛܠܝܐ: ܕܢܗܘܢ ܡܗܘܬܟܐ ܠܥܡܘܕܐ ܕܒܢ̈ܝܢܫܐ. ܘܒܪ
ܫܡܝܐ ܘܐܪܥܐ. ܝܡܐ ܘܝܒܫܐ. ܫܡܫܐ ܘܣܗܪܐ ܘܟܘ̈ܟܒܐ.

and darkness (Gen 1:4, 18), day and night (Gen 1:5, 14), wild and tame animals (Gen 1:24), creeping things and winged birds (Gen 1:20–21), and everything that goes about in the world. After all this God said to his Child and his Word, who was with him from eternity, and to the living Spirit, who completes the Trinity: '*Let us make a human being in our image, according to our likeness* (Gen 1:26), that he may be like us, and have authority over the work of our hands.' So God took dust (Gen 2:7) in his hands and fashioned and made an adult man, giving him authority (Gen 1:28) over all the things he had made. He made him dwell in the Paradise which he had planted (Gen 2:8), imposing on him ordinances to see whether or not he would keep these ordinances of his. He said, '*From all* the fruits of *the trees in Paradise you are at liberty to eat, but from the Tree of the Knowledge of Good and Evil you shall not eat, since* the moment *you do eat of it you shall* certainly *die*' (Gen 2:16–17). He also took a rib from his side and made a woman (Gen 2:21), whom he handed over to him, saying, 'She shall be your helper' (cf. Gen 2:18).

12. "Now the Evil One, seeing how much (God) loves our race, came to Eve and surreptitiously led her astray, while she in turn led Adam astray; he made her eat of the fruit of the desirable tree, and then she made Adam eat (Gen 3:1–6). Then death came to reign over his children, and so they die.

13. "When God saw that they had not kept his ordinances, he expelled them from Paradise and made them tillers upon the earth (Gen 3:23). He told them, '*Be fruitful and multiply, fill the earth and subdue it. Have dominion over the fish of the sea and the birds of the sky,* over the *wild animals* and over the *reptiles*' (Gen 1:28). Although he gave them many other good things, they forsook him, and he brought the Flood upon them, drowning them. But (God) saved Noah, his wife and children in the Ark (Gen 6).

14. "Subsequently he chose for himself as a people the seed of Abraham, providing them with laws and judicial decisions. They went down to Egypt where the Egyptians enslaved them (Exod 1:11, 14); they became workers with bricks and mud on the estates of the Egyptians, in hard labour (Exod 1:13). (God) sent them Moses, one of their own race, and he delivered them from the cruel enslavement of the Egyptians by means of the signs, miracles and mighty deeds (cf. Acts 7:36) which took place at his hands in the presence of Pharaoh, king of Egypt. He also divided the sea before them, so that they crossed over as though on dry land, while Pharaoh, who had brazenly chased after them, he drowned in the sea (Exod 14:28–9; Heb 11:29).

ܘܗܪܟܐ ܘܫܩܘܠܐ. ܐܣܩܘܠܐ ܘܠܠܐ. ܚܘܬܐ ܘܟܢܪܐ. ܪܫܝܢܐ
ܘܬܓܪܐ ܘܦܘܚܬܐ. ܘܟܠܗܝܢ ܕܐܝܬ ܕܡܬܚܫܒܢ ܒܥܠܡܐ. ܘܟܕ ܬܒܪ
ܟܠܗܝܢ ܐܡܪ ܗܘ ܐܠܗܐ ܠܫܠܝܚܗ ܘܠܬܠܡܝܕܘܗܝ ܗܘ ܕܠܘܬܗ
ܗܘܐ ܡܢ ܡܬܘܡ. ܘܪܘܚܐ ܚܝܐ ܫܘܡܠܝܐ ܕܬܫܬܘܬܐ. ܕܢܒܥܐ
ܒܪܢܫܐ ܒܝܘܡܝܢ ܐܝܟ ܕܟܬܒܬ. ܕܢܗܘܐ ܐܟܘܬܟ ܘܢܫܬܠܛ
ܒܟܒܕ ܐܬܪܝܢ. ܘܫܡܥ ܐܠܗܐ ܒܥܘܬܐ ܥܠ ܐܢܫܘܗܝ. ܘܒܟܠܗ
ܘܒܝܘܡܘܗܝ ܒܪܢܫܐ ܡܫܡܠܝܐ. ܘܐܫܬܠܛܘ ܥܠ ܟܠܗܘܢ ܒܥܒܕܘܗܝ
ܕܒܒܪ. ܘܐܫܬܡܥܘܗܝ ܒܦܘܪܫܢܐ ܗܘ ܕܢܝܚ. ܘܫܡ ܠܗ ܦܘܩܕܢܐ:
ܕܢܝܚܐ ܐܝܟܘ ܕܢܦܩ ܦܘܩܕܢܘܗܝ, ܐܘ ܠܐ. ܘܐܡܪ ܠܗ. ܕܡܢ
ܟܠܗܘܢ ܦܐܪܐ ܕܐܝܠܢܐ ܕܐܝܬ ܒܦܪܕܝܣܐ ܡܐܟܠ ܬܐܟܘܠ.
ܘܡܢ ܐܝܠܢܐ ܕܝܕܥܬܐ ܕܛܒܬܐ ܘܕܒܝܫܬܐ ܠܐ ܬܐܟܘܠ. ܡܛܠ
ܕܒܝܘܡܐ ܕܬܐܟܘܠ ܡܢܗ ܡܘܬܐ ܬܡܘܬ. ܘܫܡܥ ܐܠܗܐ ܡܢ
ܓܒܗ ܘܟܒܕܗ ܐܢܬܬܐ. ܘܐܫܠܡܗ ܠܗ ܘܐܡܪ ܠܗ. ܬܗܘܐ
ܠܟ ܗܕܐ ܡܥܕܪܢܝܬܐ.

12. ܘܚܙܝܐ ܕܚܘܝܐ ܕܟܡܐ ܪܚܡ ܠܗ ܠܓܒܪܐ. ܐܬܬ ܝܚܕ ܚܘܝܐ
ܘܐܠܒܫܗ ܠܒܒܗ. ܗܘ, ܐܠܒܫܬ ܠܐܕܡ. ܘܡܢ ܦܐܪܐ
ܕܐܝܠܢܐ ܝ ܠܓܒܟܐ ܐܘܟܠܗ: ܗܘ, ܐܘܟܠܬ ܠܐܕܡ. ܘܐܟܠܗ
ܡܘܬܐ ܥܠ ܝܠܕܘܗܝ, ܘܗܘܐ ܡܥܠܬܗ.

13. ܘܟܕ ܚܙܐ ܐܠܗܐ ܕܠܐ ܢܛܪ ܦܘܩܕܢܘܗܝ. ܐܦܩ ܐܢܘܢ ܡܢ
ܦܪܕܝܣܐ. ܘܥܒܕ ܐܢܘܢ ܦܠܚܝ ܒܐܪܥܐ. ܘܐܡܪ ܠܗܘܢ. ܦܪܘ
ܘܣܓܘ ܘܡܠܘ ܐܪܥܐ ܘܟܘܒܫܘܗ̇. ܘܫܠܛܘ ܒܢܘܢܝ ܝܡܐ
ܘܒܦܪܚܬܐ ܕܫܡܝܐ. ܘܒܚܝܘܬܐ ܘܒܪܚܫܐ. ܘܟܕ ܬܘܒ ܡܣܓܝܐ
ܠܗܘܢ ܛܒܬܐ ܛܒܘܬܗ, ܘܐܝܬ ܟܠܗܘܢ ܛܒܝܒܐ ܘܫܒܩ
ܐܢܘܢ. ܘܟܠܛ ܠܚܫ ܘܠܐܢܫܬܗ ܘܠܒܢܘܗܝ ܒܡܐܟܘܠܬܐ.

14. ܘܡܢ ܒܬܪ ܗܢܝܢ ܓܒܝܐ ܠܗ ܒܟܠܐ ܠܝܕܥܐ ܕܐܒܪܗܡ. ܘܫܡ
ܠܗܘܢ ܢܡܘܣܐ ܘܕܝܢܐ. ܘܢܣܒܘ ܠܡܨܪܝܢ ܘܥܒܕܘ ܐܢܘܢ
ܡܨܪܝܐ. ܘܗܘܘ ܦܠܚܝܢ ܒܐܪܥܐ ܕܡܨܪܝܢ. ܒܠܒܢܐ ܐܦ
ܒܛܝܢܐ. ܘܒܦܘܠܚܢܐ ܩܫܝܐ. ܘܫܕܪ ܠܡܘܫܐ ܒܪ ܥܡܪܡ.
ܘܦܪܩ ܐܢܘܢ ܡܢ ܫܘܥܒܕܐ ܩܫܝܐ ܕܡܨܪܝܐ ܒܐܬܘܬܐ
ܘܒܚܝܠܐ ܘܒܓܒܘܪܬܐ ܕܝܠܗ, ܒܐܬܘܬܗ, ܘܡܢ ܦܪܥܘܢ ܡܠܟܐ
ܕܡܨܪܝܢ. ܘܦܠܓ ܝܡܐ ܒܡܘܫܐ. ܘܥܒܪܘ ܒܗ ܐܝܟ
ܕܒܝܒܫܐ. ܘܛܒܥ ܒܗ ܦܪܥܘܢ ܕܐܪܕܦ ܒܬܪܗܘܢ.

15. "He made them dwell in the wilderness for forty years, feeding them with manna from heaven and quails from the sea, making water flow for them from a rock (Exod 16:13–17:6), while they exchanged him for another deity, casting a golden calf, in which they delighted, and which they worshipped, forgetting all the good things he had done for them (Exod 32; Ps 106:21; Acts 7:41). He then slew them, and so they turned groaning to the Lord; whereupon he delivered them, destroying instead the nations before them as they killed kings (cf. Ps 135:10, 136:16) who were hostile to them, and he handed their territories over to them.

16. "They forsook him yet again, worshipping Baal, the hosts of heaven and barren idols, the ones which you still worship today. So God sent to them his holy prophets, some of whom they sawed in half, others they stoned, others again they killed (Heb 11:37).

17. "Finally (God) sent his Son and his consubstantial Word, who was with him before he established the worlds. He supposed that they might be ashamed. So the Word came in Gabriel's mouth to Mary, a Galilean woman who belonged to their people and who was betrothed to Joseph, a descendant of David, their king (Luke 1:26–27). She, being holy and blameless, the seal of her virginity was preserved intact when the Word entered her womb, through the hearing of her ears, and became flesh in her, a perfect human being, issuing from her womb in pure fashion, her virginity untouched and preserved intact.

18. "He became a child and sucked milk, though he is the provisioner and life-giver to all created beings. He came to the Temple to the priest, to be circumcised (Luke 2:21) so that he, the giver of the Law, might fulfil the Law. He let the aged man go (Luke 2:29), releasing him from the bond that had held him until he came.

19. "He grew up among human beings and was tested by the Accuser (Matt 4:1–11), so that he might make manifest the latter's low estate and guilt. He came to baptism and was baptised at the hands of his servant in the river Jordan (Matt 3:13–17), which his own will had caused to flow.

20. "He went up with his twelve disciples whom he had chosen so that they might proclaim his Gospel to the world. He embarked on a ship so that they might cross to the other side (of the lake), and on board he dozed off to sleep (Matt 8:24)—though still being awake and governing both heaven and earth. He walked over the waves of the sea, stretching out a hand to Simon, to draw him out of the sea, then walking with him across the water to the other side (Matt 14:26–32).

15. ܘܐܫܪܝ ܐܢܘܢ ܒܡܕܒܪܐ ܐܪܒܥܝܢ ܫܢܝܢ. ܟܕ ܡܬܪܣܐ ܠܗܘܢ
ܒܡܢܢܐ ܡܢ ܫܡܝܐ. ܘܣܠܘܝ ܡܢ ܝܡܐ. ܘܐܪܕܝ ܠܗܘܢ ܡܝܐ ܡܢ
ܟܐܦܐ. ܘܗܢܘܢ ܣܠܩܘܗܝ ܠܐܠܗܐ. ܘܥܒܕܘ ܠܗܘܢ ܥܓܠܐ
ܕܕܗܒܐ. ܘܣܓܕܘ ܠܗ ܘܕܒܚܘ ܠܗ. ܘܦܠܚܘ ܠܟܠܗܝܢ ܦܬܟܪ̈ܐ
ܕܚܕܪ ܠܗܘܢ. ܘܩܛܠ ܐܢܘܢ. ܘܦܢܘ ܘܬܒܘ ܠܘܬ ܡܪܝܐ. ܘܦܪܩ
ܐܢܘܢ. ܘܦܢܐ ܘܥܒܪ ܚܛ̈ܗܐ ܡܢ ܦܪܨܘܦܗܘܢ. ܘܡܛܠܠ ܡܠܟܐ
ܒܥܠܕܒ̈ܒܝܗܘܢ ܘܝܗܒ ܠܗܘܢ ܐܪ̈ܥܬܗܘܢ.

16. ܘܬܘܒ ܠܟܐܘܗܝ, ܘܫܠܡܗ ܠܒܒܠ. ܘܠܫܒܝܬܐ ܕܫܒܝܐ.
ܘܠܦܬܟܪ̈ܐ ܚܪ̈ܢܐ. ܗܠܝܢ ܕܠܗܘܢ ܣܓܕܝܢ ܐܢܘܢ ܥܡܡܐ.
ܘܫܪܝ ܠܬܘܗܘܢ ܒܢܘܗܝ, ܡܕ̈ܝܢܬܐ: ܘܡܢܗܘܢ ܢܦܩܘ ܘܡܢܗܘܢ
ܪ ܓܒܐ. ܘܡܢܗܘܢ ܡܝܬܘ.

17. ܘܠܚܪܬܐ ܫܕܪ ܠܒܪܗ ܘܠܡܠܬܗ ܒܪ ܚܝܢ. ܗܘ ܕܐܬܓܠܝ,
ܗܘܐ ܒܒܗܡ ܡܢ ܡܪܝܡ ܕܢܬܝܢ ܫܠܝܚܐ. ܘܐܡܪ ܒܪܐ ܒܟܬܝܒ.
ܐܬܐ ܗܒܠ ܡܠܬܐ ܒܦܘܡܗ ܕܓܒܪܐܝܠ ܠܘܬ ܡܪܝܡ
ܒܬܘܠܬܐ ܒܪܬ ܒܝܬܗܘܢ. ܗܝ ܕܡܟܝܪܐ ܗܘܬ ܠܝܘܣܦ ܒܪ
ܕܘܝܕ ܡܠܟܗܘܢ. ܘܒܪ ܡܫܝܚܐ ܘܠܝܬ ܒܗ̇ ܡܘܡܐ. ܘܫܠܝܡ
ܘܡܠܝ ܠܟܠܗ̇ ܕܒܬܘܠܘܬܗ̇. ܟܠ ܡܠܬܐ ܠܒܪܣܗ̇ ܡܢ ܫܡܥܐ
ܕܐܕ̈ܢܝܗ̇. ܘܗܘܐ ܒܗ̇ ܒܣܪܐ ܒܪܢܫܐ ܡܫܠܡܢܐ. ܘܢܦܩ ܡܢ
ܡܪ̈ܚܡܗ̇ ܕܒܬܘܠܬܐ ܟܕ ܒܬܘ̈ܠܝܗ̇ ܠܐ ܐܫܬܪܝܘ ܘܠܐ ܐܬܦܬܚܘ.

18. ܘܗܘܐ ܡܠܘܕܐ ܘܥܡܗ ܫܠܝܚܐ ܟܕ ܗܘ ܡܫܒܚ ܘܢܗܒ ܚܝ̈ܠܐ
ܠܟܠܗܘܢ ܒ̈ܢܝܬܐ. ܐܬܐ ܠܡܚܠܡܐ ܠܗܘܢ ܒܗܘܢܐ. ܘܐܬܓܒܪ
ܕܢܚܠܐ ܢܚܘܫܐ ܗܘ ܡܫܘܚܗ ܕܢܚܘܫܐ. ܘܫܪܐ ܠܡܫܥܒܕܘܬܐ
ܡܢ ܐܣܘܪ̈ܐ ܕܐܣܪܗ̇ ܒܗ ܐܬܐ.

19. ܘܐܬܪܒܝ ܒܢܫܬ ܒܢܝ̈ܢܫܐ. ܘܐܬܚܙܝ ܡܢ ܐܟܠܘܣ̈ܐ. ܕܢܣܒܘܗܝ,
ܥܡܠܗ ܘܫܘܒܚܬܗ. ܘܐܬܐ ܠܥܡܕܐ ܘܐܬܥܡܕ ܡܢ ܐܝܕ̈ܝ,
ܒܪܗ ܕܟܘܗܢܐ ܢܒܝܐ ܕܐܪ̈ܙܐ ܝܘܚܢܢ.

20. ܘܓܒܐ ܡܢ ܬܠܡܝܕܘܗܝ ܬܪ̈ܥܣܪ ܕܢܟܪܙܘܢ ܠܗ. ܕܢܒܪܘܢ ܡܟܪܙܘܬܗ
ܒܥܠܡܐ. ܘܫܠܡ ܠܡܫܝܚܘܬܐ ܕܢܟܪܙܘܢ ܠܟܪܙܐ. ܘܝܗܒ ܘܐܘܕܥ ܒܗ
ܒܝܬ ܘܡܒܪܟ ܠܥܡܡܐ ܘܠܐܪܥܐ. ܘܫܠܡ ܥܠ ܓܠܠܐ ܕܥܡܡܐ.
ܘܝܗܒ ܐܚܕܐ ܠܥܡܡܐ. ܘܕܠܝܗ ܡܢ ܡܝܐ. ܘܫܠܡ ܒܗܘ
ܘܒܪܐ ܠܒܪܝܬܐ.

21. "When tribute money was required, he gave orders to a fish to provide a stater from the sea; this he then handed over on behalf of himself and Simon (Matt 17:27). He opened the eyes of the blind, cleansed the lepers, caused the deaf to hear, while the dumb spoke and the dead were revived. From the edge of his garment he gave healing to the infirm body of a woman who had been tormented by a haemorrhage for twelve years (Matt 9:20); he drove out from a girl a demon which had been tormenting her for a long time (cf. Matt 9:24–25); he caused a paralyzed man, who had been lying in affliction for thirty-eight years, to stand up (John 5:5–8); he drove out a legion of demons from another man, causing them to enter some swine, and drowning them in the sea (Matt 8:28–34); he rebuked a fever, and it left the body (Matt 8:14–15). He manifested miracles which belong to his divinity, calling out to Lazarus and raising him from the grave after four days (John 11:38–44). Likewise, out of five loaves and two fishes he satisfied the hunger of many thousands (Matt 14:17–21).

22. "After all these miracles which no tongue can recount, the Jews arrested him out of envy (cf. Matt 27:18), because they knew that he was the Son of God. They took him before Pilate the governor, and put him on trial, scourging him. Pilate, seeing that there was not a single reason why he should be put to death, washed his hands and said, "*I am guiltless of the blood of this* man" (Matt 27:24). Nevertheless they condemned to death him who dies not. They crucified him on a piece of wood, and placed a crown of thorns (Mark 15:17) on the head of him who binds the crowns of kings. He asked for water on the cross (John 19:28), he who causes springs and rivers to flow; they offered him vinegar and bitter herbs (John 19:29). All this happened so that the words which the prophets had spoken concerning him might not prove false (cf. Acts 3:18), to make known that he had put on a body, like us.

23. "After this he cried out on the cross to his Father, '*El, El, why have you forsaken me*' (Matt 27:46). Nature, whether silent or endowed with a voice, shook: the sun hid its light, shaking at the voice of its Lord; the moon and the stars were hidden, and there was a great darkness from the sixth to the ninth hour (Matt 27:45). The rocks split and the graves were opened: the dead arose and gave praise to him for their deliverance. The Temple veil was torn from top to bottom (Matt 27:51–52).

21. ܘܐܬܬܟܒ ܒܥܘ ܪܫܐ. ܦܩܕ ܠܗܘܢܐ ܘܐܦܩ ܐܣܛܪܛܐ ܡܢ
ܡܚܐ. ܘܢܗܒ ܚܠܦܘܗܝ ܘܚܠܦ ܫܒܩܘܗܝ. ܦܬܚ ܩܫ̈ܬܐ. ܕܒܝ
ܓܒܪܐ. ܐܫܡܕ ܕܘ̈ܓܒܐ. ܡܠܠܘ ܚܪ̈ܫܐ. ܚܙܘ ܡܢܬܐ. ܢܗܒ
ܡܢ ܒܥܘܗ ܚܘܠܡܢܐ ܠܓܘܫܡܐ ܡܚܝܠܐ ܕܐܬܬܢܬ ܕܢܘܠܬܗ̇
ܡܕܝܢܬܐ ܕܕܡܐ ܫܢ̈ܝܐ ܬܬܪܒܘܪܐ. ܓܪ ܫܐܕ̈ܐ ܡܢ ܓܠܝܬܐ
ܕܢܘܠܬܗ̇ ܢܓܪܐ ܦܓܫܐܐ. ܐܣܝܩ ܠܡܫܪܢܐ ܕܕܡܐ ܗܘܐ
ܬܠܬܝܢ ܘܬܪ̈ܬܝܢ ܫܢܝܢ ܒܐܘܠܝܢܐ. ܓܪ ܠܓܘܢܐ ܕܫܐܕܪܐ ܡܢ
ܓܒܪܐ. ܘܐܟܠ ܐܢܘܢ ܒܚܢܪܐ. ܘܚܝܡ ܐܢܘܢ ܓܒܗ ܡܚܐ.
ܟܐܒ ܒܐܫܬܐ ܘܟܪܘܬ ܡܢ ܦܓܪܐ. ܚܘ ܚܝܠܐ ܕܐܠܗܘܬܗ.
ܡܐܐ ܠܠܒܪ ܘܐܘܣܒܗ ܡܢ ܓܘ ܡܟܪܒ ܠܐܪܒܥܐ ܢܦ̈ܫܢ. ܘܡܢ
ܚܡܫܐ ܠܚܝ̈ܢ ܘܬܪܝܢ ܢܦܫܐ. ܗܘܘ ܐܠܦܐ ܦܓ̈ܥܐ.

22. ܘܡܢ ܒܬܪ ܗܠܝܢ ܚܝܠܐ ܕܠܐ ܡܫܬܚܪ ܦܘܡܐ ܕܢܡܠܠ ܐܢܘܢ.
ܐܚܪ̈ܢܐ, ܢܬܪ̈ܐ ܒܫܘܒܚܗܘܢ. ܒܠ ܕܢܕܒܘ ܕܗܘܘ ܒܪܗ
ܕܐܠܗܐ. ܘܡܪܒܘܗܝ, ܠܗܬ ܦܠܛܘܣ ܐܝܓܡܘܢܐ ܘܕܢܘܗܝ,
ܘܝܓܕܘܗܝ, ܘܚܙܐ ܦܠܛܘܣ ܕܠܗܬ ܒܗ ܚܙܐ ܒܠܬܐ ܕܫܦܪܐ
ܠܡܘܬܐ: ܘܐܫܬܟܚ ܐܢܪ̈ܘܗܝ, ܘܐܡܪ. ܕܐܢܐ ܡܚܣܢ ܐܢܐ ܡܢ
ܕܡܗ ܕܓܒܪܐ ܗܢܐ. ܗܘܘ ܕܝܢ ܚܝܒܘܗܝ, ܠܡܘܬܐ. ܠܗܘ̇
ܕܠܐ ܡܟܐܬ. ܘܙܩܦܘܗܝ, ܒܠ ܩܝܣܐ. ܘܗܡܒ ܠܗ ܒܠܝܠܐ ܕܟܘ̈ܟܒܐ
ܒܪܫܗ: ܠܗܘ̇ ܕܦܓܪ ܗ̈ܓܒܐ ܕܬ̈ܠܒܐ. ܫܐܠ ܡܢܐ ܒܪܩܦܐ. ܗܘ̇
ܕܡܪܕܐ ܢܒ̈ܝܐ ܘܢܣܪܘܬܐ: ܘܡܪܒܘ ܠܗ ܚܝܠܐ ܘܡܕܪ̈ܪܐ. ܗܠܝܢ
ܒܠܗܝܢ ܕܠܐ ܢܛܪ̈ܬܒܠ ܬ̈ܠܐ ܕܢܒ̈ܝܐ ܕܡܠܠܘ ܒܠܗܘܢ, ܕܢܘܕܒ
ܕܦܓܪܐ ܕܐܒܘܬܢ ܠܒܫ.

23. ܘܒܬܪ ܗܠܝܢ ܡܒܐ ܒܪܡܫܐ ܠܗܬ ܐܒܘܗܝ, ܐܟܠ ܐܟܠ ܠܡܒܢܐ
ܫܒܘܬܢ. ܘܪܒܘ ܒܢܝܢܐ ܫܬܡܫܐ ܘܡܬܠܠܐ. ܫܡܫܐ ܚܦ ܢܗܘܪܗ
ܕܪܒ ܡܢ ܡܠܐ ܕܡܕܘܪܗ. ܗܘܪܐ ܘܒܘܟ̈ܒܐ ܐܬܚܫܟܘ. ܘܗܘܐ
ܚܫܘܟܐ ܪܒܐ ܡܢ ܫܬܐ ܫܥܐ ܒܕܡܐ ܠܬܫܥ. ܘܦܘܩܒܘ ܗܘܘ
ܫܒܝ̈ܠܐ ܘܐܬܦܬܚܘ ܡܕܪ̈ܐ. ܘܩܡܒܘ ܡܢܬܐ: ܘܫܒܚܘܗܝ, ܒܠ
ܦܘܪܩܢܗܘܢ. ܐܝܟܢܐ, ܐܦ ܬܪܒܐ ܕܗܡܒܠܐ ܡܢ ܠܒܠ ܒܕܡܐ
ܠܬܚܬ.

24. "After all these signs which he performed the stony heart was not softened; instead, they acted all the more audaciously, piercing his side with a spear, whereupon there came forth blood and water (John 19:34)—water for baptism and blood for our drink, just as he told his disciples in the Upper Room before he suffered, when he ate the Passover with them, broke bread and gave it to them saying, '*Take, eat, this is my body*, and *this is my blood which is* given *for many for the forgiveness of* debts and *sins*' (Matt 26:26–29). (This was the time) when he drove his cunning betrayer from their midst (John 13:27), revealing to them concerning his passion, death and resurrection.

25. "After they had pierced him in his side and he had shown his disciples the truth of his words when he said that his blood would be shed, he died in a way that only he knows, of his own will. They laid him in a new tomb and set guards to watch it (Matt 27:60, 66). After three days he arose, and he manifested himself to his disciples after his resurrection, showing them his hands and feet and the place where he had been wounded by the sword (John 20:20).

26. "After his resurrection he was in the world for forty days (Acts 1:3). He gave instructions to his disciples and told them, 'Go out, *instruct and baptize all peoples in the name of the Father and the Son and the Holy Spirit* (Matt 28:19). He who believes and is baptized and *confesses me before men* shall live, and *I will confess him before my Father who is in heaven* and before all his angels; *but he who* does not believe and *denies me before men, him will I too deny before my Father who is in heaven* (Matt 10:32–33), and before his angels' (Luke 9:26). He also said to them, '*All that* you *shall bind on earth shall be bound in heaven, and what* you *loose on earth shall be loosed in heaven*' (Matt 16:19). He further said, 'Behold, I shall ascend to my Father, and once I have ascended to him I will send you the Spirit, the Paraclete, from my Father's presence; he will confirm you in the truth' (John 14:26; 15:26).

27. "He ascended in glory to heaven to his Father who had sent him, and he sits at the right hand of his Father. We are dying for his sake, but sword, fire, combings, fetters, tortures, sufferings and death, all kinds of afflictions, cannot separate us from his truth (cf. Rom 8:35).

28. "These few things have I recounted to you, but once you have been baptized and come to know God, you will read about them and learn of all their significance. But now, for the present, as for the request you made to your Lord that he show you his mysteries, it was for this very reason that he sent me, with instructions to baptize you."

24. ܘܡܢ ܒܬܪ ܗܠܝܢ ܐܬܘ̈ܬܐ ܕܚܙܐ. ܠܒܐ ܕܟܐܦܐ ܠܐ ܐܬܪܟܢ.
ܐܠܐ ܡܬܪܐܡ ܗܘܐ ܒܡܪܚܘܬܗܘܢ܆ ܘܕܘܪܘܗܝ، ܒܕܦܢܗ
ܒܠܗܘܬܐ. ܘܢܦܩ ܡܢܗ̇ ܕܒܚܐ ܘܢܟ̈ܣܐ. ܡܢܐ ܠܒܝܬܐ ܘܕܒܚܐ
ܠܥܡܘܬܗܘܢ. ܐܝܟ ܕܐܡܪ ܠܬܠܡܝܕܘܗܝ، ܒܥܠܬܐ ܗܕܡ ܕܚܙܐ: ܒܗ
ܐܒܠ ܒܒܝܬܗܘܢ ܦܪܝܫܐ. ܘܩܪܐ ܠܚܒܪܐ ܘܝܗܒ ܠܗܘܢ ܘܐܡܪ
ܠܗܘܢ. ܣܒܘ ܐܟܠܘ. ܗܢܘ ܦܓܪܝ، ܘܗܢܘ ܕܡܝ: ܕܢܣܒ
ܡܬܝܗܒܐ ܠܫܘܒܩܢܐ ܕܚܘ̈ܒܐ ܘܕܚܛ̈ܗܐ. ܘܦܩܕ
ܠܢܚܠܐ ܡܫܠܡܢܗ ܡܢ ܒܝܬܗܘܢ. ܘܐܙܠ ܠܗܘܢ ܥܠ ܚܫܗ
ܘܒܝܬܗ ܘܡܫܒܚܬܗ.

25. ܘܡܢ ܒܬܪ ܕܕܘܪܗܝ، ܒܕܦܢܗ. ܘܫܘܝ، ܠܬܠܡܝܕܘܗܝ، ܫܕܪܐ ܕܒܠܬܗ
ܕܐܡܪ ܠܗܘܢ ܕܢܬܟܢܫ ܡܢܬ. ܐܝܟ ܕܗܘ ܢܕܒ
ܡܢ ܒܝܬܗ: ܘܡܥܡܕܗ، ܒܒܝܬ ܡܥܡܘܪܐ ܚܕܬܐ. ܘܐܡܫܚܗ ܢܦܘܪ̈ܐ
ܕܢܛܘܪܝܗ، ܘܠܬܠܬܐ ܢܩ̈ܦܝܢ ܥܡ. ܘܫܘܝ، ܢܦܩܗ ܠܬܠܡܝܕܘܗܝ، ܡܢ
ܒܬܪ ܡܫܒܚܬܗ. ܘܫܘܝ، ܐܚܘܗܝ، ܘܪ̈ܒܝܗܘܢ، ܘܕܘܒܪܬ ܙܘܡܪܐ
ܕܟܠܗ.

26. ܘܗܘܐ ܒܠܠܝܐ ܐܪ̈ܒܥܝܢ ܝܘ̈ܡܝܢ ܒܬܪ ܡܥܡܕܝܬܗ. ܘܦܩܕ
ܠܬܠܡܝܕܘܗܝ، ܘܐܡܪ ܠܗܘܢ. ܦܘܩܘ ܬܠܡܕܘ ܘܐܥܡܕܘ ܥܡ̈ܡܐ
ܟܠܗܘܢ. ܒܫܡ ܐܒܐ ܘܒܪܐ ܘܪܘܚܐ ܩܕܝܫܐ. ܡܢ ܕܡܗܝܡܢ
ܘܥܡܕ ܡܘܕܐ ܒܝ ܩܕܡ ܒܢ̈ܝܢܫܐ ܚܝܐ. ܘܐܢܐ ܡܘܕܐ ܐܢܐ
ܒܗ ܩܕܡ ܐܒܝ ܕܒܫܡܝܐ. ܘܩܕܡ ܟܠܗܘܢ ܡܠܐܟ̈ܘܗܝ، ܘܡܢ
ܕܠܐ ܡܗܝܡܢ ܘܟܦܪ ܒܝ ܩܕܡ ܒܢ̈ܝܢܫܐ. ܟܦܪ ܐܢܐ ܐܦ ܐܢܐ ܒܗ
ܩܕܡ ܐܒܝ ܕܒܫܡܝܐ ܘܩܕܡ ܡܠܐܟ̈ܘܗܝ، ܘܐܡܪ ܠܗܘܢ ܕܟܠܡܐ
ܕܬܐܣܪܘܢ ܒܐܪܥܐ ܢܗܘܐ ܐܣܝܪ ܒܫܡܝܐ. ܘܡܕܡ ܕܬܫܪܘܢ
ܒܐܪܥܐ ܢܗܘܐ ܫܪܐ ܒܫܡܝܐ. ܘܐܡܪ ܠܗܘܢ. ܕܗܐ ܐܙܠ
ܐܢܐ ܠܘܬ ܐܒܝ. ܘܡܐ ܕܐܙܠܬ ܠܘܬܗ: ܡܫܕܪ ܐܢܐ ܠܟܘܢ
ܪܘܚܐ ܦܐܪܩܠܝܛܐ ܡܢ ܠܘܬ ܐܒܝ. ܕܗܘ ܢܥܕܪܟܘܢ ܒܥܕܪܐ.

27. ܘܣܠܩ ܒܫܘܒܚܐ ܠܫܡܝܐ ܠܘܬ ܐܒܘܗܝ، ܕܫܕܪܗ: ܘܝܬܒ ܡܢ
ܝܡܝܢܐ ܕܐܒܘܗܝ، ܘܫܠܡ ܡܕܒܪܢܘܬܗ ܡܫܡܠܝܬܐ. ܘܫܘܒܚܐ ܘܝܩܪܐ
ܘܬܘܕܝܬܐ ܘܐܝܩܪܐ ܘܫܘܒܚܐ ܘܡܘܕܝܢܘܬܐ ܘܥܠ ܐܠܦܝ̈ܢ
ܠܐ ܦܪܫܝܢ ܠܝ ܡܢ ܚܘܒܗ.

28. ܗܠܝܢ ܐܬܘ̈ܬܐ ܬܫܥܝܬ ܠܟ. ܘܡܟܐ ܕܝܢ ܕܒܡܕܝܢܬ ܘܡܕܝܢܬ
ܠܐܠܗܐ. ܦܪܫܬ ܒܗܠܝܢ. ܘܢܦܩܬ ܟܠܗ ܚܝܠܗܘܢ܀ ܗܫܐ ܕܝܢ
ܡܛܠ ܗܢ̈ܝ ܫܐܠܬܐ ܕܫܐܠܬ ܡܢ ܡܪܢ ܕܢܚܘܝܢ ܐܪ̈ܙܘܗܝ܇ ܘܥܠ
ܗܢ̈ܝ ܫܪ̈ܝܪܝܢ ܘܦܩܕܢܝ ܕܐܒܕܝܢ܀

29. When the blessed Mar Maʿin heard this from the holy Benjamin he fell down on his face in front of him, saying, "I confess God almighty, who has not acted with me as my sins deserve, but he has immediately hastened to send you and to effect my salvation at your hands. What now hinders my baptism? (cf. Acts 8:36) Henceforth nothing can separate me from the truth of God and the love of our Lord Jesus Christ" (cf. Rom 8:35).

30. On seeing that he believed with his whole heart, the blessed Benjamin got up at once and went off to a spring of water which issued from there. He then baptized the holy Mar Maʿin; and because he had received the priesthood from the holy Barse, bishop of Edessa, the city of Mesopotamia, once he had baptized him, he also took bread and wine and consecrated them, whereupon the two of them partook of the Body of our Lord. He then brought the Scripture, opened it and read out to him, explaining to him the passages from it concerning Christ, thus strengthening him in faith in our Lord.

31. On bidding him farewell he said, "Remain in peace, my brother, now that our Lord has wished to turn you to the New Life. Remain and watch over yourself lest you be caught in the snare of the Evil One, the Adversary, either by reason of your money, or through beatings, tortures and afflictions, resulting in your denying the truth you have acknowledged, and trampling on his Body and Blood which you have this day received. Look at what Paul, the builder of the Church, says in the Letter to the Hebrews: 'If he *who transgresses the Law of Moses is put to death without mercy* (Heb 10:28), how much more he who has trampled on the Body of God and considered the Blood of his Testament to be like that of any man.' It is not the body and blood of a mortal man which you have received: you should not think of it as bread and wine, but as the Body of Jesus Christ, the Son of God, by which all your sins have been wiped out. Preserve your baptism without stain; fight the good fight (1 Tim 6:12), like a true soldier of Jesus Christ, so that you may be held worthy to hear his voice which says, '*Come, blessed ones of my Father, inherit the Kingdom which* is prepared *for you* from *before the foundations of the world*'" (Matt 25:34).

32. Having instructed him carefully, he said, "I am leaving you now. King Shapur will come to hear of all this and will send men to kill me in my cell. You he will treat harshly and put on trial, but God will shortly effect

29. ܘܟܕ ܗܠܝܢ ܫܡܥ ܛܘܒܢܐ ܡܪܝ ܡܥܝܢ ܡܢ ܩܕܝܫܐ ܒܢܝܡܝܢ. ܢܦܠ ܥܠ ܐܩ̈ܠܘܗܝ ܩܕܡܘܗܝ, ܘܐܡܪ ܠܗ. ܡܘܕܐ ܐܢܐ ܠܐܠܗܐ ܐܚܝܕ ܟܠ. ܕܠܐ ܥܒܕ ܥܡܢ ܐܝܟ ܚܛ̈ܗܝܢ. ܐܠܐ ܒܓܠܠ ܛܘܒܗ ܘܥܕܪܢܝ ܘܥܒܕ ܠܝ ܦܘܪܩܢܐ ܒܝܕ ܐܝ̈ܕܝܟ. ܘܗܫܐ ܡܢܐ ܗܝ ܥܠܬܐ ܕܐܬܝܬ. ܕܡܢ ܗܫܐ ܠܝܬ ܡܕܡ ܕܦܪܫ ܠܝ ܡܢ ܥܘܕܪܗ ܕܐܠܗܐ. ܘܫܘܟܢܗ ܕܡܪܢ ܝܫܘܥ ܡܫܝܚܐ.

30. ܘܟܕ ܚܙܐ ܛܘܒܢܐ ܒܢܝܡܝܢ ܕܗܝܡܢ ܠܗ ܡܢ ܟܠܗ ܠܒܗ. ܩܡ ܡܫܪܐ ܘܐܙܠ ܠܥܝܢܐ ܕܡ̈ܝܐ ܕܢܦܩܐ ܡܢ ܬܡܢ ܘܐܥܡܕܗ ܠܩܕܝܫܐ ܡܪܝ ܡܥܝܢ. ܘܡܛܠ ܕܡܥܡܘܕܝܬܐ ܡܫܡܠܝܐ ܗܘܬ ܠܗ ܡܢ ܩܕܝܫܐ ܒܪܘܚܐ ܐܦܝܣܩܘܦܐ ܕܐܘܪܗܝ, ܒܡܕܝܢܬܐ ܕܒܝܬ ܢܗܪ̈ܝܢ. ܘܟܕ ܐܥܡܕܗ ܢܣܒ ܠܚܡܐ ܘܚܡܪܐ ܘܩܕܫ ܐܢܘܢ ܘܫܡܠܝ ܬܪ̈ܝܗܘܢ ܦܓܪܗ ܕܡܪܢ. ܘܐܬܝܗ, ܟܠܬܐ ܘܦܬܟ ܘܡܪܐ ܩܕܡܘܗܝ. ܘܦܩܕ ܠܗ ܡܢܗ ܥܠ ܡܫܝܚܐ. ܘܫܪܪܗ ܒܗܝܡܢܘܬܐ ܕܡܪܢ.

31. ܘܝܗܒ ܠܗ ܫܠܡܐ ܘܐܡܪ ܠܗ. ܐܙܠ ܦܘܫ ܒܫܠܡܐ. ܗܫܐ ܕܟܝܐ ܡܪܢ ܘܐܦܨܝܟ ܠܒܢܝܐ ܚܐܪܬܐ: ܦܘܫ ܘܚܝ, ܢܦܫܟ ܕܠܐ ܬܬܚܫ ܒܦܣܘܗ ܕܒܫܝܐ ܒܠܕܪܐ. ܐܘ ܒܟܠܬ ܡܪ̈ܗܛܝܟ. ܐܘ ܒܡܚܫܘܬܐ ܕܥܒܕ̈ܐ ܘܐܘܠܨ̈ܢܐ. ܕܬܬܟܦܪ ܒܥܒܕܐ ܕܐܘܪܚܬ ܒܗ: ܘܬܕܘܥ ܦܓܪܗ ܘܕܡܗ ܐܝܢܐ ܕܥܠܬ ܘܡܫܝܚܐ. ܚܝ, ܡܢܐ ܐܢܐ ܐܡܪ ܡܫܝܚܐ ܕܝܬܪܐ ܦܘܠܘܣ ܒܐܓܪܬܐ ܕܒܪ̈ܝܢܐ. ܕܐܝܟ ܡܢ ܗܘ̇ ܕܐܟܠ ܥܠ ܢܦܫܗ ܕܗܘܝܐ ܕܠܐ ܙ̈ܕܩܝܢ ܡܢܐܬ. ܚܝ ܒܚܝܐ ܐܢܐ ܕܢܫܟܗ ܠܦܓܪܗ ܕܐܠܗܐ: ܘܫܬܐ ܕܡܗ ܕܐܫܬܦܟ ܕܠܗ ܐܝܟ ܕܦܠܝܫ. ܠܘ ܒܪ ܦܓܪܐ ܘܕܡܐ ܕܒܪܢܫܐ ܡܝܘܬܐ ܢܣܒܬ. ܘܠܐ ܠܚܡܐ ܘܚܡܪܐ ܬܫܡܫܬܗ; ܐܠܐ ܦܓܪܗ ܕܡܫܝܚܐ ܡܫܝܚܐ ܒܪܗ ܕܐܠܗܐ. ܕܒܗ ܐܬܟܪܙܘ ܟܠܗܘܢ ܢܒ̈ܝܐ. ܐܦ ܡܫܡܫܢܘܬܟ ܕܠܐ ܛܘܠܫܐ. ܐܝܟܢܐ ܫܦܝܪܐ ܐܬܬܡܫ: ܐܝܟ ܦܠܚܐ ܫܦܝܪܐ ܕܝܫܘܥ ܡܫܝܚܐ. ܕܬܫܡܫܬܐ ܕܬܫܡܫ ܡܠܗ ܕܐܡܪ. ܬܘ ܒܪ̈ܝܟܘܗܝ ܕܐܒܝ ܝܪܬܘ ܡܠܟܘܬܐ ܗ̇ܝ ܕܡܛܝܒܐ ܠܟܘܢ ܡܢ ܩܕܡ ܬܪܡܝܬܗ ܕܥܠܡܐ.

32. ܘܟܕ ܦܩܕܗ ܘܙܗܪܗ ܗܠܝܢ: ܐܡܪ ܠܗ. ܗܐ ܐܢܐ ܐܙܠ ܐܢܐ ܠܝ ܡܢ ܠܘܬܟ. ܘܟܠܗܘܢ ܗܠܝܢ ܫܡܥܬ ܥܒܕܬ ܡܠܟܐ ܘܡܫܕܪ ܘܡܛܠ ܠܝ ܒܝܕܗ ܡܠܟܐ, ܘܠܝ ܐܠܨ ܠܝ ܒܕܝܢܐ ܡܫܚܐ. ܐܠܐ ܒܓܠܠ ܚܕ ܠܝ ܐܠܗܐ ܦܘܪܩܢܐ ܘܠܟܠܗ ܒܕܬܗ ܒܝܕ

your rescue, and that of all his Church, at the hands of the believing man, the victorious king who is in the Roman realm (*Romania*). But have no fear, you shall die in the true faith somewhere else. Farewell."

33. After (Benjamin) had given his blessing and departed, king Shapur went down to visit one of the cities of his dominion and asked for Ma'in, but failed to find him. He summoned the nobles of his realm and said to them, "Where is my general, Ma'in? For it has been a few days now that I have not seen him; maybe he has gone off to some distant place, but if so, why did he not confer with me and notify me?"

34. The nobles replied, "By your life, O king, not even those of his own household know where he is, and now he has been away eight days. No riding animal went with him, and he did not take any of his servants apart from a Christian (*naṣraya*) boy from the desert of Dura who was instructing him in the Christian religion. He must be still there."

35. The king at once sent a considerable number of horsemen after him, telling them, "Even if you have to wander through all the mountain country as far as Roman territory, do not come back without bringing him."

36. The men set off for the mountain region, and circulating all over it, they came upon the cave where they found him kneeling in prayer facing the east. The Marzban who had gone after him addressed him, "Ma'in, get up and come along: the king is asking for you. You have been denounced before him for being a Christian." The blessed man replied, "Yes, indeed, you are quite right, I am a Christian, that is, if Christ holds me worthy to depart from the world with this name."

37. He got up in haste and set off with them to king Shapur. The king glared at him in anger, and before he had time to prostrate himself in the customary manner, said to him, "Yes, foolish Ma'in, just because I gave you a position of honour in my kingdom, appointing you a general in my presence, and exalting you, do you now despise me and refuse to prostrate yourself before me? Tell me now, is it true what I have heard about you, that you are a Christian?" The blessed man replied, "Yes, it is quite true, I am a Christian, a servant of our Lord Jesus Christ."

ܟܒܪܐ ܡܗܝܡܢܐ ܡܠܟܐ ܕܟܢܐ ܗܘܐ ܒܪܘܡܝܐ. ܐܠܐ ܠܐ
ܬܕܚܠ ܕܐܢܬ ܒܡܗܝܡܢܘܬܐ ܕܫܪܪܐ ܡܛܠ ܐܢܬ ܒܐܬܪܐ
ܐܚܪܢܐ. ܐܠܐ ܦܘܫ ܒܫܠܡܐ܀

33. ܒܗ ܕܝܢ ܒܪܗ ܘܦܪܫ ܡܢܗ܆ ܢܣܒ ܫܒܘܪ ܡܠܟܐ ܕܢܐܙܠ ܠܚܕܪܐ
ܡܢ ܩ̈ܪܝܬܐ ܕܫܘܠܛܢܗ. ܘܒܥܘܗܝ ܠܡܥܝܢ ܘܠܐ ܐܫܟܚܘܗ.
ܘܩܪܐ ܠܚܐܪܐ ܕܡܠܟܘܬܗ ܘܐܡܪ ܠܗܘܢ. ܐܝܟܘ ܡܥܝܢ ܪܒ
ܚܝܠܐ ܕܝܠܝ܆ ܕܗܐ ܝܘܡܝܢ ܬܠܬܐ ܕܠܐ ܐܬܚܙܝ ܠܝ.
ܕܠܡܐ ܠܕܘܟܐ ܐܚܪܢܐ ܐܙܠ. ܠܡܢܐ ܕܝܢ ܐܦ ܐܙܠ ܠܐ
ܐܬܡܠܟ ܒܝ ܘܫܐܠܢܝ.

34. ܐܡܪܝܢ ܠܗ ܚܐܪܐ. ܠܐ ܝܕܥܝܢ ܕܝܠܢ ܡܠܟܐ܆ ܕܐܦܠܐ ܒܬܪ
ܒܬܠܬܗ ܝ̈ܘܡܝܢ ܒܗ ܐܝܟܘ܆ ܘܡܢ ܗܘܐ ܘܩ̈ܛܠܬܐ ܬܡܝܗܬܐ. ܠܐ
ܫܘܝܬܐ ܟܪ ܐܢܫ ܒܗܘܢ܆ ܘܠܐ ܡܢ ܒܢ̈ܝܗܘܢ ܕܒܪ ܒܗܘܢ.
ܐܠܐ ܐܦ ܒܠܚܘܕܝܗ ܚܕ ܢܘܪܐ ܡܢ ܡܕܒܪܐ ܕܕܘܪܐ ܕܡܬܠܡܕ
ܗܘܐ ܠܗ ܠܕܝܠܬܐ ܕܢܘܪܐ. ܘܗܘܐ ܬܡܢ ܗܘ ܒܕܒܝܠ܀

35. ܘܫܕܪ ܒܬܪܗ ܡܫܕܪܐ ܡܠܟܐ ܐܢܫܐ ܦܪ̈ܫܐ ܠܐ ܙܥܘܪ. ܘܐܡܪ
ܠܗܘܢ ܡܠܟܐ. ܒܟܠܗ ܛܘܪܐ ܐܦ ܦܫܘܢ ܐܢܬܘܢ ܒܥܘܐ
ܠܫܘܠܛܢܐ ܕܪ̈ܘܡܝܐ. ܕܠܐ ܐܫܬܘܕܝܬܘܢܝ ܠܗ ܠܐ ܬܐܬܘܢ.

36. ܗܝܕܝܢ ܢܦܩܘ ܐܢܫܐ ܗܠܝܢ ܠܛܘܪܐ. ܘܗܘܘ ܡܬܒܪܝܢ ܒܗ.
ܘܟܠܗ ܠܗ̇ ܡܕܒܪܬܐ. ܘܐܫܟܚܘܗܝ، ܒܗ ܫܥܬܐ ܒܘܪܟܐ ܠܡܕܒܚܐ
ܘܡܩܪܒܐ. ܘܒܢܐ ܡܕܒܚܐ ܗܘ ܕܗܘܐ ܒܬܪܗ ܘܐܡܪ ܠܗ. ܡܢܝܢ
ܗܘܐ ܫܥܬܐ. ܗܐ ܡܠܟܐ ܒܥܐ ܠܟ. ܕܬܩ̈ܪܒ ܐܬܐܟܠ
ܡܕܝܢܬܐ، ܕܢܘܪܐ ܐܢܬ܀ ܒܢܐ ܛܘܒܢܐ ܘܐܡܪ ܠܗܘܢ. ܐܝܟ
ܒܢܘܪܐ ܫܦܝܪ ܐܡܪܬܘܢ ܕܢܘܪܐ ܐܢܐ. ܐܦ ܡܫܝܚܐ ܠܝ
ܡܫܝܚܐ ܕܒܗܘܢ ܫܒܩܐ ܐܦܘܗܝ ܡܢ ܒܠܡܐ.

37. ܘܡܢ ܡܣܪܗܒܐܝܬ ܘܢܣܒ ܒܚܝܠܗܘܢ ܠܘܬ ܡܠܟܐ ܫܒܘܪ. ܘܚܙܐ
ܒܗ ܡܠܟܐ ܒܫܠܡܬܐ. ܒܕܠܐ ܢܦܠ ܣܓܕ ܠܗ ܐܝܟ ܥܒܕܐ.
ܘܐܡܪ ܠܗ. ܐܝܟ ܣܟܠܐ ܡܥܝܢ܆ ܟܠ ܕܝܗܒܬ ܠܟ ܐܝܩܪܐ
ܒܡܠܟܘܬܝ܆ ܘܒܥܕܬܟ ܪܒ ܚܝܠܐ ܥܒܕܟ ܘܐܘܪܒܬܟ܆ ܡܛܠ
ܡܢܐ ܫܒܩܬܢܝ ܘܠܐ ܣܓܕܬ ܠܝ. ܗܫܐ ܐܡܪ ܠܝ. ܒܢܘܪܐ
ܐܢܬܘܢ، ܡܕܡ ܕܫܡܥܬ ܥܠܝܟ ܕܢܘܪܐ ܐܢܬ܀ ܛܘܒܢܐ ܐܡܪ.
ܐܝܟ ܒܢܘܪܐ ܢܘܪܐ ܐܢܐ. ܒܒܪܗ ܕܡܪܝ ܢܫܒܚ ܡܫܝܚܐ܀

38. The tyrant said, "And were you not previously a Magian, and a chief Magian at that?" The blessed man said, "I was a Magian, a confederate of Satan. But ever since Christ wanted to take me to himself and make me a Christian by name, I shall not depart from him, even in the face of death, for I am his servant for ever."

39. The pagan said, "What has happened to you, Ma'in? Up to now you hated the Christians, instructing me in all sorts of bitter deaths and cruel tortures for them, and now you are confessing their teaching, declaring that you are a servant of their god. Just listen to me and worship the sun and moon, the governors of the world, just as you formerly used to. Worship the mighty fire which is never put out, and sacrifice to Zeus the great god, to Nanai the great goddess of all the earth, and to Nabu and Bel, the powerful gods. Renounce that Nazarene you have confessed: he cannot save you from my hands. Furthermore, inform me who is the sorcerer who has come along and deceived you, turning you into a Christian?"

40. The holy man answered him, "Previously I did persecute the Christians, since I had gone astray after those gods whom you have just mentioned in front of me. But when I saw and learnt that the sun is just a created object and that the moon and stars have an overlord, and that each has received exact instructions not to transgress his proper boundary (Ps. 104:9), and that the one cannot oppress the other, but sometimes the moon is bigger, and sometimes it is smaller, and sometimes again the two are equal, without the one oppressing its mate—Yes, when I understood and became aware of this gentle Lord, I followed after him, and I am ready to die for his sake, for I have discovered that it is a good and fine thing to die for him. And because in the past I used to cause hurt to his servants, today I am requesting them to make intercession with him on my behalf, asking that he may give me the strength and endurance to bear up under tortures and afflictions for his name's sake, and that I may be victorious when I have to enter battle with you.

41. "If only I was in a position to force everyone, with tears and groans and supplication, to confess his name, just as hitherto I used force on those who confessed his name. Not that he has any need of me to bring people to the worship of him, but to make up for having made many deny his name, I should like to bring many to his worship; for he wishes for

38. ܐܡܪ ܠܗ ܓܝܘܪܐ. ܘܠܐ ܡܓܘܫܐ ܗܘܝܬ ܥܕܡܐ ܠܗܫܐ
ܘܪܫܐ ܕܡܓܘܫ̈ܐ܀ ܐܡ̇ܪ ܠܗ ܓܝܘܪܐ. ܡܓܘܫܐ ܗܘܝܬ ܘܒܪ
ܡܠܟܗ ܕܦܪܣܝܐ. ܘܡܢ ܕܝܕܥܬ ܒܗ ܒܡܫܝܚܐ ܕܒܪܬ ܠܐܠܗܗ ܘܥܒܕܬ
ܢܘܪܐ ܡܫܡܫܬܐ. ܘܥܕܡܐ ܠܡܘܬܐ ܠܐ ܡܫܥܢܐ ܐܢܐ ܡܢ
ܠܗܘܬܗ. ܐܠܐ ܗܘܐ ܐܢܐ ܠܗ ܥܒܕܐ ܠܥܠܡ܀

39. ܐܡܪ ܠܗ ܣܗܕܐ. ܡܢܐ ܗܘܐ ܠܟ ܡܥܝܢ: ܕܗܘܐ ܥܕܡܐ
ܠܡܘܡܢܐ ܦܢܐ ܗܘܝܬ ܠܢܘܪܐ. ܘܡܫܡ̈ܫܬܐ ܡܬܪ̈ܢܐ ܡܠܟ ܗܘܝܬ
ܠܗ ܒܠܥܕܘܗܝ. ܘܐܘܠܨ̈ܢܐ ܡܫ̈ܢܐ. ܘܗܫܐ ܡܥܕܪܐ ܐܢܬ
ܒܥܠܕܒܒܘܗܝ. ܘܐܡܪܬ ܐܢܬ ܕܥܒܕܗ ܐܢܐ ܕܐܠܗܗܘܢ. ܐܠܐ
ܫܒܚܝܢ ܘܣܓܕܝܢ ܠܫܡܫܐ ܘܠܣܗܪܐ ܡܕܒܪ̈ܢܘܗܝ ܕܥܠܡܐ. ܐܝܟ
ܥܒܕܐ ܡܕܡܝܐ. ܘܠܢܘܪܐ ܚܝܘܬܐ ܕܠܐ ܪܥܝܐ. ܘܥܒܕܝܢ ܠܗܘܢ
ܐܠܗܐ ܪܒܐ. ܘܠܝܢ ܐܠܗܘܬܐ ܪܒܬܐ ܕܟܠܗ ܐܪܥܐ. ܘܠܒܢܘ
ܘܠܟܠ ܐ̈ܠܗܐ ܛܥܝܘܬܐ. ܘܒܗܘܪ ܒܗܘ ܢܘܪܐ ܕܐܘܕܝܬ ܒܗ:
ܕܠܐ ܡܥܒܕ ܦܘܡ ܠܟ ܡܢ ܐܟܘܢ. ܘܬܘܒ ܕܝܢ ܐܡܪ ܩܕܡܟ ܕܡܢܘ
ܗܘ ܚܫܐ ܕܐܬܐ ܥܠܝܟ ܘܐܬܦܠܓܬ ܘܥܒܕܟ ܢܘܪܐ܀

40. ܩܕܝܫܐ ܕܝܢ ܥܢܐ ܘܐܡܪ ܠܗ. ܡܢ ܩܕܝܡ ܪܕܦ ܗܘܝܬ ܠܟܪ̈ܣܛܝܢܐ
ܥܠ ܕܛܥܝܬ ܒܬܪ ܗܠܝܢ ܕܐܬܝܠܕܬ ܩܕܡܝ. ܘܟܕ ܚܙܝܬ ܘܠܒܫܬ
ܕܡܫܝܚܐ ܒܟܢܫܐ ܗܘ: ܘܗܝܡܢܐ ܘܡܥܡܕܢܐ ܕܡܪܝܐ ܐܝܬ ܠܗܘܢ.
ܘܡܬܦܩܕܘ ܡܬܦܩܕܝܢ. ܘܚܙܝ ܡܢܗܘܢ ܬܫܡܫܬܗ ܠܐ ܥܒܪ. ܘܚܙܝ
ܠܚܕ ܕܢܥܒܕܘܢ ܠܐ ܡܨܝܢ. ܐܠܐ ܐܝܬ ܐܡܬܝ, ܕܢܬܒ ܗܢܐ
ܘܢܬܒ ܗܢܐ. ܘܐܝܬ ܐܡܬܝ ܕܥܒܕܝܢ ܬܫܡܫܬܗܘܢ: ܘܠܐ ܟܠ ܚܕ
ܡܢܗܘܢ ܠܚܒܪܗ. ܘܟܕ ܢܟܬ ܘܐܪܓܫܬ ܒܗܢܐ ܡܪܐ ܒܫܡܝܐ
ܐܙܠܬ ܒܠܒܗ. ܘܫܠܦܬܘܢ, ܐܢܐ ܡܢܝܬ ܐܢܐ. ܕܢܟܬ ܕܥܬܝܕ ܗܘ
ܘܠܟ ܠܐܒܕ ܕܢܗܘܬ ܡܛܠܠܬܗ. ܘܕܐܬܠܝ ܗܘܝܬ ܠܒܢܝܗܘܢ: ܗܐ
ܗܘܡܢܐ ܒܢܟܐ ܐܢܐ ܡܢܗܘܢ: ܕܒܒܗܬܐ ܥܠ ܐܦ̈ܝ ܢܒܥܘܢ
ܡܢܗ. ܕܢܬܠ ܠܝ ܚܝܠܐ ܘܡܫܝܢܘܬܐ ܕܐܫܡܥܪ ܥܒ̈ܕܐ
ܘܐܘܠܨ̈ܢܐ ܡܛܠ ܥܡܗ. ܘܐܡܪܬ ܒܥܝܢ ܘܐܡܪܝܢ܀

41. ܘܐܬܚܫܒ ܕܝܢ ܐܡܝܢ ܕܐܬܠܝ ܗܘܝܬ ܥܕܡܐ ܠܡܘܡܢܐ ܠܐܟܠܝܡ
ܕܡܕܝܢ ܗܘܘ ܒܥܡܗ. ܫܠܦܬ ܗܘܝܬ ܗܫܐ ܕܐܠܘܝ ܒܕ̈ܡܟܐ
ܘܒܫܘܟܠܐ ܘܒܒܗܬܐ ܠܚܠܨ ܕܢܘܕܐ ܒܥܡܗ. ܠܐ ܕܚܫܝܡ ܥܠܝ
ܕܐܬܐ ܐܢܫܐ ܠܡܟܬܒܗ. ܐܠܐ ܫܠܦ ܕܡܟܦܪ ܗܘܝܬ
ܠܡܓ̈ܢܐ ܒܥܡܗ: ܐܬܐ ܡܓ̈ܢܐ ܠܡܟܬܒܗ. ܗܘ ܒܪ
ܝܘܡܐ ܒܫܢܐ ܕܠܗܘܢ ܒܫ̈ܒܥܐ. ܘܬܪܐܬ ܕܝܢ ܕܡܗ̈ܡܢܐ.

the salvation of everyone, but particularly of believers. And I am confident in my Lord that he will help me and that I shall turn to him a hundred times as many as those who apostasized, not just in this country, but also in each of the lands of the other peoples. The person who instructed me and baptized me told me all this, and I am convinced that it was the truth that he spoke."

42. The king said, "I will have you put to death by burning, seeing that it is the Fire which you have denied. In this way the words of that deceiver who led you astray will come to nothing, for you will not escape from my hands. But tell me who this man is, and I will show how he can save himself from my hands!"

43. The blessed man replied, "He told me himself at the time that he would die at your hands. His name is Benjamin, and he is living in the desert of Dura, where he has performed numerous miracles. He is just as eager in his mind for death as I am now. Nevertheless I am confident his words will not prove false."

44. The king answered, "Yes, by the unquenchable Fire, I will carry out his wishes immediately, and don't you be so sure that you will escape from my hands!"

45. He straightaway gave orders, "Let Ma'in, who has rebelled against me and insulted me, by despising my gods, receive a good scourging; then let them rub vinegar, salt and asafoetida into his wounds. Then have him confined in the law court until I have consulted with the nobles what to do with him. As for Walgash the Marzban, my orders are that he should take some troops and go and search out the deceiver Benjamin: whoever finds him is to kill him, and prevent him from making anyone else rebel against the king."

46. Without delay they swiftly carried out the king's orders. Now at that time there happened to be an ambassador from the Romans with king Shapur. He was someone with a firm belief in Christ and had been sent by the believing emperor Constantine to make peace with Shapur and to receive tribute from him. Shapur had received him with magnificence, giving him gifts and numerous tokens of honour; he even gave him a royal crown to take back to his master, the believing emperor.

ܘܬܟܝܠ ܐܢܐ ܥܠ ܡܪܝ ܕܡܥܕܪ ܠܝ. ܘܡܫ̈ܟܚܐ ܒܩܝܡ ܥܠ ܐܘܠܨ
ܕܒܥܘ ܒܗ ܡܩܒܠܐ ܐܢܐ ܠܘܬܗ. ܠܐ ܒܗܢܐ ܐܬܪܐ ܒܠܚܘܕ:
ܐܠܐ ܒܟܠ ܐܬܪ̈ܘܢ ܕܒܡ̈ܕܝܢܬܐ ܐܚܪܢܐ. ܗܘ ܓܝܪ ܕܐܬܠܒܒܢܝ
ܘܐܚܒܒܢܝ: ܗܘ ܐܡܪ ܠܝ ܗܠܝܢ. ܘܡܫܪܪ ܐܢܐ ܠܟ ܕܫܪܝܪܐ ܗܝ
ܡܠܬܐ ܕܐܡܪܬ܀

42. ܐܡܪ ܠܗ ܡܠܟܐ. ܗܐ ܒܝܘܡܐ ܡܬܠ ܐܢܐ ܠܟ: ܒܗܝ ܕܒܥܘܬ
ܒܗ. ܐܝܟܢܐ ܕܬܫܬܪܪ ܡܠܬܗ ܕܗܘ ܡܦܝܣܢܐ ܕܐܦܝܣܟ: ܕܡܢ
ܐܝܕܝ ܠܐ ܦܠܛ ܐܢܬ. ܐܡܪ ܠܝ ܕܝܢ ܡܢܘ. ܘܐܝܢܐ ܐܠܗܐ
ܐܝܟܢܐ ܡܦܠܛ ܢܦܫܗ ܡܢ ܐܝܕܝ܀

43. ܠܘܩܒܠܐ ܕܝܢ ܐܡܪ ܠܗ. ܐܦ ܗܘ ܗܟܝܠ ܐܡܪ ܠܝ ܡܢܘ ܕܒܢܝܐ
ܕܟܠ ܐܪ̈ܥܢ ܡܠܟܐ. ܐܝܬܘܗܝ ܕܝܢ ܥܡܪܗ ܒܫܡܝܐ. ܘܐܝܬܘܗܝ
ܒܡܕܝܢܬܗ ܒܡܕܒܪܐ ܕܕܘܪܐ. ܐܝܟܢܐ ܕܫܒܩܠܐ ܙܘܕܩܐ ܒܒܪ ܒܗܘ
ܡܕܒܪܐ. ܘܐܝܟ ܕܦܫܩ ܐܢܫ ܕܠܐ ܡܫܐ ܠܡܘܬܐ. ܗܟܢܐ
ܐܦ ܐܢܫ ܕܠܗ ܡܫܒܚ ܠܗ ܠܡܘܬܐ. ܒܪܡ ܕܝܢ ܬܟܝܠ ܐܢܐ
ܕܡܠܬܗ ܠܐ ܡܬܕܒܠܐ܀

44. ܥܢܐ ܡܠܟܐ ܘܐܡܪ ܠܗ. ܐܝܟ ܢܘܪܐ ܕܠܐ ܕܥܟܐ ܐܢܐ ܐܘܩܕ
ܒܟ ܡܚܒܠܐ. ܘܗܕܐ ܕܦܠܛ ܐܢܬ ܡܢ ܐܝܕܝ ܠܐ ܬܬܚܫܒ܀

45. ܘܦܩܕ ܡܚܒܠܐ ܕܢܚܡܘܢ ܕܡܪܕ ܥܠܝ ܘܢܟܪܢܝ ܘܥܒܕ ܠܐܠܗܗ. ܢܬܠܚܕ
ܙܪܝܙܐܝܬ. ܘܢܪܡܘܢ ܚܠܐ ܘܡܠܚܐ ܘܫܠܦܬܐ ܥܠ ܡܚ̈ܘܬܗ.
ܘܢܬܡܫܟ ܒܟܠ ܕܢܐ ܒܕܡܐ ܕܢܦܩ ܐܢܐ ܡܠܟܐ ܡܢ ܚܐܪ̈ܐ
ܕܡܢܐ ܐܚܪܢ ܠܗ. ܘܠܘܩܒܠ ܡܪܘܒܢܐ ܦܩܕ ܐܢܐ ܠܗ ܕܢܦܩ
ܫܠܝܐ ܘܐܙܠ ܢܚܡܘܗܝ، ܠܦܠܚܐ ܒܫܡܝܢ. ܘܥܠ ܕܢܥܒܕܘܢ
ܢܦܠܛܘܗܝ. ܕܠܐ ܢܗܘܐ ܡܥܕܪ ܐܢܫܐ ܡܢ ܡܠܟܐ.

46. ܘܡܚܒܠܐ ܥܒܕܘ ܐܝܟ ܕܐܡܪ ܡܠܟܐ ܘܠܡܠܟܘܬܐ. ܒܗܘ ܕܝܢ ܙܒܢܐ
ܐܝܬ ܗܘܐ ܚܕ ܐܝܟ ܒܪܕܐ ܡܢ ܙܪ̈ܥܝܐ ܠܒܝܬܗ ܕܫܒܘܪ ܡܠܟܐ.
ܘܦܠܚ ܡܗܝܡܢ ܗܘܐ ܒܟܢܫܝܐ. ܕܫܒܘܪܗ ܗܘܐ ܡܠܟܐ
ܡܗܝܡܢܐ ܘܡܫܠܛܢܘܬܐ. ܕܒܒܪ ܫܢܝܐ ܥܡ ܫܒܘܪ. ܘܢܦܩ
ܒܗܝ ܡܕܝܢܬܐ. ܘܡܠܠܗ ܫܒܘܪ ܡܠܟܐ ܙܪܝܙܐܝܬ: ܘܕ̈ܝܢܐ
ܘܐܘܡ̈ܢܐ ܙܪܝܙܐ ܢܦܩ ܗܘܐ ܠܗ. ܘܐܦ ܬܒܥܐ ܕܡܠܟܘܬܐ
ܢܦܩ ܠܗ. ܕܢܗܘܐ ܠܡܪܗ ܡܠܟܐ ܡܗܝܡܢܐ.

47. When this believer saw the distress with which his Christian coreligionists were afflicted there, and saw how Mar Ma'in was mercilessly flogged, he went back and told the victorious emperor, Constantine, his master, informing him of all that he had beheld, and about Mar Ma'in. The emperor was greatly distressed, and wept, refusing any food on that day. So affected by grief was he that he spent the night fasting in sympathetic mourning for the servants of God. He fell down and lay (lit. slept) on sackcloth and ashes, supplicating Christ for his fellow-believers, asking that they be not further afflicted.

48. In the morning he sent for and collected together all the sons of Marzbans who were hostages with him. He had them confined and treated badly, while to the wicked king he sent missives full of angry threats, as follows:

49. "If you do not release all the Christians you have shut up in prison, and in particular your general, Ma'in, who is greatly oppressed, I will put to death the sons of your nobles who are here with me, and I will send you their heads. I will also annul the treaty which exists between you and me, and I will invade your whole country, causing destruction and devastation. I will pursue you and kill you; I will dismember you limb by limb, and not a hair from the head of anyone will escape, without my cutting off your limbs with the sword."

50. The young boys also wrote letters to their families informing them of the hardships imposed upon them by the emperor. The emperor then gave the letters to this believer, telling him, "Do not return from there before all the Christians who are incarcerated are released from prison, and (before Shapur) and his nobles put down in writing that anyone who oppresses or kills the Christians shall be required to pay three thousand pounds (*litra*) of gold. As for the blessed old man Ma'in, escort him out in honour, and if he wants to, let him come and live with me in honour. But if he is going to stay there, give him my royal seal, so that he may travel about without fear."

47. ܘܟܕ ܚܙܐ ܗܘܐ ܗܢܐ ܡܗܝܡܢܐ ܠܒܢ̈ܝ ܕܚܠܬܐ ܕܐܠܗ ܒܪܕܘܦܝܐ ܕܟܐܝܢܐ ܐܘܠܨܢܐ ܒܟܕܝܢ ܗܘܘ: ܘܚܙܝܗ، ܠܗ ܠܡܪܝ، ܡܥܝܢ ܕܐܡܝܢܐ ܚܠܦ ܕܠܐ ܦܘܫܐ: ܫܠܚ ܘܐܡܪ ܠܗ ܠܡܠܟܐ ܕܟܠܐ ܡܪܗ ܡܡܫܡܫܢܘܬܗ ܘܐܫܬܥܒܕ ܠܗ ܥܠ ܕܨܒܐ. ܘܡܛܠܬܗ ܕܡܪܝ، ܡܥܝܢ. ܘܐܬܬܥܝܩ ܡܠܟܐ ܫܦܝܪ ܘܒܟܐ. ܘܠܐ ܐܟܠ ܠܚܡܐ ܒܝܘܡܐ ܗܘ. ܐܠܐ ܗܘܢܐ ܡܢ ܒܥܘܬܗ ܒܗ ܕܠܐ ܡܐܒܠܘܬܐ ܡܢ ܐܟܠܗ ܘܫܬܝܗ ܕܟܠ ܒܢ̈ܘܗܝ، ܕܐܠܗܐ. ܘܟܠ ܘܕܡܟ ܥܠ ܣܩܐ ܘܩܛܡܐ: ܟܕ ܡܦܝܣ ܠܡܫܝܚܐ ܥܠ ܒܢ̈ܝ ܗܝܡܢܘܬܗ ܕܠܐ ܬܘܒ ܢܬܐܠܨܘܢ❖

48. ܘܡܢ ܦܪܐ ܫܕܪ ܘܩܪܐ ܠܟܠܗܘܢ ܒܢ̈ܝ ܡܕܝܢܬܐ ܕܐܝܬ ܗܘܘ ܗܦܪ̈ܟܐ ܠܬܚܬܗ. ܘܩܪܐ ܐܢܘܢ. ܘܐܠܦ ܐܢܘܢ. ܘܦܩܕ ܠܗ ܠܡܠܟܐ ܒܟܠܗ ܐܓܪܬܐ ܕܩܕܝܡ ܗܘܐ ܘܠܘܬ ܢܦܫܗ ܗܢܐ.

49. ܕܐܢܫܘ ܕܠܐ ܬܦܩ ܠܟܠܗܘܢ ܒܪܕܘܦܝܐ ܕܡܫܡܫܝܢ ܠܝ ܒܡܫ̈ܡܫܢܐ. ܡܬܛܪܐܕܬ ܕܝܢ ܠܡܥܝܢ ܪܒ ܚܝܠܐ ܕܐܠܗܝ. ܐܢܫܐ ܕܡܢ ܐܠܗܝ. ܒܢ̈ܝ ܚܐܪ̈ܝ ܕܐܝܬ ܠܘܬܝ، ܐܦܠܐ ܘܐܫܕܪ ܠܝ ܪ̈ܡܫܝܗܘܢ. ܘܡܫܝܚܐ ܐܢܫܐ ܕܐܝܬ ܗܘܐ ܒܗܬ ܠܝ ܘܠܝ ܐܫܪܐ. ܘܐܬܪܝ ܟܠܗ ܐܘܚܕܬ ܐܬܪܘܬ ܘܐܘܬܒ. ܘܐܪܕܦܝ ܘܠܝ ܐܦܠܠܝ. ܗܪܕ ܗܪܕ ܐܦܩܘܗܝ. ܠܐ ܕܝܢ ܡܛܠܬܐ ܡܢ ܪܥܝܐ ܕܚܙ ܡܢܗܘܢ ܬܦܠܟܐ. ܘܐܠܐ ܒܫܦܝܐ ܡܦܠܒ ܐܢܐ ܗܪܕܡܝܢ.

50. ܘܐܦ ܗܠܝܢ ܬ̈ܠܬܐ ܬܘܒ ܟܬܒ ܐܓܪܬܐ ܠܐܚ̈ܝܢܘܗܝ ܘܐܘܕܥ ܐܢܘܢ ܥܠ ܐܘܠܨܢܐ ܗܘ ܕܥܒܕ ܠܗܘܢ ܡܠܟܐ. ܘܡܛܠ ܐܝܟ ܡܠܟܐ ܠܐ ܐܓܪܬܐ ܠܡܗܝܡܢܐ ܗܘ ܘܐܡܪ ܠܗ ܕܠܐ ܬܫܡܥ ܡܢ ܬܘܒ ܕܠܐ ܢܦܫܘܢ ܟܠܗܘܢ ܒܪܕܘܦܝܐ ܗܠܝܢ ܕܡܫܡܫܝܢ ܟܘܬ ܡܫ̈ܡܫܢܐ. ܘܥܒܕ ܠܝ ܗܘ ܘܐܚ̈ܘܗܝ، ܕܟܠ ܕܐܠܗܝ ܘܟܠ ܕܡܛܠ ܠܒܪܕܘܦܝܐ: ܢܗܘܘܢ ܡܬܬܥܝܩܝܢ ܬܠܬܐ ܐܝ̈ܟܝܢ ܠܡܠ̈ܟܝܢ ܕܗܟܢܐ. ܘܠܗܘ ܦܘܠܚܢܐ ܗܟܢܐ ܡܥܝܢ: ܐܦܩܘܗܝ، ܒܐܡܘܪܐ. ܘܐܢ ܒܥܐ ܢܬܬܐ ܠܗ ܚܕ، ܘܬܒ ܒܐܡܘܪܐ. ܘܐܢ ܬܗܘܐ ܦܓܥ: ܗܒ ܠܗ ܚܬܡܐ ܕܡܠܟܘܬܝ، ܕܢܗܘܐ ܡܗܠܟ ܕܠܐ ܕܚܠܐ❖

51. The faithful man took the letter and set off, accompanied by the power of God as he went on his way.

52. The tyrannical Marzban came and found the blessed Mar Benjamin, and once he had put him to death, he returned to the king. On hearing of the blessed Mar Benjamin's death, Mar Ma'in was exceedingly grieved.

53. That same night the blessed man appeared to him and said, "Do not grieve, my brother, for my request has been fulfilled, and my Lord has rewarded me for my toil. You too shall have respite in a few days time, and you will be delivered in great glory, both you and all the true believers who are imprisoned and afflicted in every region of Shapur's dominion." He then laid his hand on (Ma'in's) wounds and they were immediately healed, as though no harm had come upon him. He was then whisked away (cf. Acts 8:39), and was raised up from him.

54. Now king Shapur became involved in the clash of war with the Greeks who wanted to go up against him. There was a period of about fifty days during which he did not have time to judge the case of the holy Mar Ma'in, but after fifty days when he was free to do so, he got rid of (other) obstacles and sent for Mar Ma'in; he had him brought before him, and said to him,

55. "Well, Ma'in, will you sacrifice to the gods and worship sun and fire? Will you return to your former position of honour? Or are you still sticking to your old stubbornness? If you perform my will, then your latter honour will be even greater than your former, and I shall give you presents, excellent tokens of honour, and silver and gold. But if you refuse, I will make you an object of mockery and terror to all who behold you; with your example I will put fear into all the nobles, so that they do not imitate you and go astray, abandoning the gods."

56. The holy man answered, saying, "(My) body is delivered over into your hands; destroy it as you will. Over my soul, however, you have no authority. I am confident in the Lord God that he will effect my deliverance today, rescuing me from your filthy hands, you evil and wicked man, Satan's confederate."

57. Hearing these words of abuse, Shapur gave orders that he be hung up and the (torture) combs be applied. They strung him up and applied the combs mercilessly upon the old holy man in the middle of the town.

51. ܫܡܥ ܕܝܢ ܡܗܝܡܢܐ ܗܘ̇ ܠܐܓܪܬܐ ܘܚܙܐ. ܟܕ ܠܘܐ ܠܗ
ܚܝܠܗ ܕܐܠܗܐ̇ ܘܐܬܐ ܗܘܐ ܒܐܘܪܚܗ܀

52. ܗܘ ܕܝܢ ܡܢܘܒܐ ܓܘܪܐ ܐܙܠ ܘܐܫܬܥܝܗ ܠܩܕܝܫܐ ܡܪܝ ܒܢܝܡܝܢ
ܘܩܛܠܗ ܘܚܠܦ ܠܘܬ ܡܠܟܐ. ܘܟܕ ܫܡܥ ܡܪܝ ܡܥܝܢ ܕܐܬܩܛܠ ܠܗ
ܩܕܝܫܐ ܡܪܝ ܒܢܝܡܝܢ ܐܬܬܥܝܩ ܛܒ ܠܒ܀

53. ܘܒܗ ܒܠܠܝܐ ܐܬܚܙܝ ܠܗ ܓܒܪܐ ܘܐܡܪ ܠܗ. ܠܐ ܬܬܥܝܩ
ܐܚܝ. ܐܢܐ ܓܝܪ ܐܫܬܐܠܬ ܕܝܠܟ ܐܫܬܡܠܝܬ. ܘܐܓܪܐ
ܕܥܡܠܟ ܦܫ ܠܟ ܡܪܝ. ܘܐܦ ܠܝ ܟܕ ܢܦܩܬܐ ܡܠܠ ܗܘ̇ܐ ܠܝ
ܢܦܫܐ ܘܡܬܦܪܢܣܬ ܒܥܘܒܕܐ ܪܒܐ ܐܢܬ ܘܟܠܗܘܢ ܡܗܝ̈ܡܢܐ
ܥܬ̈ܝܪܐ ܕܣܒܝܢ ܘܐܠܝܨܝܢ ܒܟܠ ܐܬܪ̈ܘܢ ܕܡܠܟܘܬܗ ܕܫܒܘܪ.
ܘܗܫܐ ܐܢܕܗ ܟܠ ܡܫܘܬܗ ܘܡܣܒܪܐ ܐܬܗܠܟ. ܐܝܟ ܗܘ
ܕܒܢܫܐ ܡܕܡ ܠܐ ܡܬܠܝܡ. ܘܐܬܓܢܢ ܘܐܬܛܠܠ ܡܢܗ܀

54. ܫܡܥܘ ܕܝܢ ܡܠܟܐ ܢܦܠ ܒܬܟܫܐ ܕܡܪܟܐ ܕܩܝ̈ܢܐ ܕܟܒܘ
ܕܢܗܘܘܢ ܟܠܗܘܢ. ܘܗܘܐ ܒܗ ܢܦܩܬܐ ܐܝܟ ܣܓܝ̈ܐܢ ܘܠܐ
ܐܫܬܟܚ ܕܢܗܘܢܗܘܢ ܠܩܕܝܫܐ ܡܪܝ ܡܥܝܢ. ܘܡܢ ܒܬܪ ܣܓܝ̈ܐܢ
ܝܘ̈ܡܝܢ ܕܐܫܬܟܚ. ܫܕܪܗ ܠܢܦܫܐ ܘܥܕܪ ܒܬܪ ܡܪܝ ܡܥܝܢ
ܘܐܝܬܝܗ ܩܕܡܘܗܝ ܘܐܡܪ ܠܗ.

55. ܟܕ ܚܙܐ ܡܥܝܢ. ܡܫܒܚ ܐܢܬ ܠܐܠܗܐ ܘܦܩܕ ܐܢܬ ܠܡܫܬܐܠܘ
ܘܢܘܪܐ. ܘܦܢܐ ܐܢܬ ܠܐܣܘܪܝ ܩܕܡܝܟ. ܐܘ ܟܕܟܠ
ܒܡܪܘܬܟ ܩܕܡܬܐ ܡܗܘܐ ܐܢܬ. ܘܐܟܢܝ ܬܟܒ ܠܝ ܒܝܢܬܐ
ܢܗܘܐ ܐܣܘܪܝ ܐܚܪܢܐ ܬܐܪ ܡܢ ܩܕܡܝܟ. ܘܟܪ̈ܝܐ ܘܐܣܘܪܐ
ܬܠܝܐ. ܘܡܐܡܪܐ ܘܕܘܒܪܐ ܐܬܠ ܠܝ. ܘܐܟܢܝ ܠܐ. ܐܡܪܬܝ
ܒܝܬܐ ܘܡܘܙܕܪܐ ܠܟܠܗܘܢ ܚܝ̈ܠܝ. ܘܐܟܪܙ ܒܝ ܠܟܠܗܘܢ
ܚܐܪܐ ܕܬܗܘܐ ܗܘܢ ܐܡܪܬܝ ܠܐ ܢܦܩܘܢ ܘܠܐ̈ܠܗܐ ܠܐ
ܢܦܩܘܢ܀

56. ܟܕܐ ܩܕܝܫܐ ܘܐܡܪ ܠܗ. ܦܓܪܐ ܡܫܠܡ ܒܐܝܕܝܟ. ܐܝܟ
ܕܟܢܫܬ ܐܘܟܪܝܣܗ. ܟܠ ܢܦܫ ܕܝܢ ܠܝܬ ܠܝ ܫܘܠܛܢܐ. ܬܟܝܠ
ܐܢܐ ܥܠ ܡܪܢܐ ܐܠܗܐ ܕܗܘܟܢܐ ܟܕܪ ܠܝ ܦܘܪܩܢܐ. ܘܡܦܩܝܐ
ܠܝ ܡܢ ܐܝܕܝܟ ܓܝܚܬܐ. ܪܫܝܥܐ ܒܥܫܐ ܟܪ ܡܠܟܘܬܗ ܕܫܠܝܛܐ.

57. ܘܟܕ ܡܠܟ ܝܢܒܪܐ ܫܡܥ ܫܒܘܪ. ܦܩܕ ܕܢܬܬܠܐ ܘܢܫܬܪܘܫ.
ܘܬܐܠܗܘܗܝ، ܘܦܘܪܩܘܗܝ، ܕܠܐ ܚܘܣ ܠܦܓܪܐ ܩܕܝܫܐ. ܒܟܝܚܠܬܗ

While this was still happening, a horseman entered and informed the king that the believer of the emperor of the Romans had arrived. Just as the king was wanting to get up to receive him, as though through God's working, (the envoy) quickly entered—to find the holy man hung up on some wood in the middle of the town in the process of having the combs applied. He dismounted from his horse and went up and kissed his feet. He then gave orders that he be taken down from the wooden frame, whereupon he immediately gave the letter from the believing emperor to Shapur and to all the nobility of his kingdom. On reading this, Shapur shook with fear, all the more so because the believer had seen the blessed man under torture. He was also afraid lest the nobles rise up against him on account of their children and kill him because they had heard how they were in distress, (subjected) to harsh judgement.

58. Then that believer addressed him, "Look at what our great emperor writes to you: send and have released all the Christians who have been imprisoned by you, wherever it may be; and free this holy man, so that he can go off wherever he likes. For my lord gave me instructions that, if he wishes to return with me, he will accord to him his due honour there. So if he wishes to come with me, let him do so without fear; but if he wishes to remain, let no one touch him. If a single hair of his head goes missing, then whatever he wrote to you will truly be put into effect."

59. Shapur then gave orders that heralds should cry out in every town that anyone who oppresses or harms one of the Christians, or who says anything evil and hateful to them, shall have his head removed by the sword. Rather, everyone should honour and reverence them. Thereupon the faithful rejoiced that our Lord had granted them their requests in all the churches, without fear.

60. Annoyed in his heart that he had not put the holy man to death, and afraid because of the letters from the victorious emperor, Shapur gave instructions in writing as follows: men and women, all with censers and bright torches, should go in front of the blessed man as far as his palace, and he would invite them, along with him, to eat with him.

61. But the holy man did not want this, and said, "Far be it from me, by the Lord God, that I should eat food with the foul man." Nevertheless that believer persuaded him, and he ate with him just bread and cheeses and dried fish that had come with him from the west.

ܕܡܕܝܢܬܐ. ܘܟܕ ܬܠܬܐ ܘܡܣܬܪܘ: ܦܪܫܐ ܥܠ ܘܐܘܕܥ ܠܡܠܟܐ
ܕܡܗܝܡܢܐ ܕܡܠܟܐ ܕܪ̈ܘܡܝܐ ܐܬܐ. ܘܟܕ ܚܙܐ ܡܠܟܐ ܕܢܣܩ
ܢܡܠܟܘܗܝ̣ ܐܝܟ ܕܡܢ ܡܕܒܪܢܘܬܐ ܕܐܠܗܐ. ܥܠ ܠܓܘ ܠܓܘ
ܘܐܫܟܚܗ ܠܡܪܝܫܐ ܟܕ ܬܠܐ ܒܡܫܚܐ ܒܡܨܥܬ ܡܕܝܢܬܐ
ܘܡܫܬܘܪ. ܘܢܣܒ ܡܢ ܫܘܫܦܐ ܘܐܙܠ ܢܫܩ ܪ̈ܓܠܘܗܝ. ܘܦܩܕ
ܘܐܚܬܘܗܝ ܡܢ ܩܝܣܐ. ܘܡܚܝܕܐ ܢܗܒ ܐܓܪܬܐ ܕܡܠܟܐ
ܡܗܝܡܢܐ ܠܥܒܕܐ ܘܠܟܠܗܘܢ ܚܐ̈ܪܝ ܡܠܟܘܬܗ. ܘܟܕ ܩܪܐ ܐܢܘܢ
ܥܒܕܘ ܐܝܟ ܘܕܝܠ. ܬܬܪܐܡܬ ܥܠ ܕܝܢܗ، ܡܗܝܡܢܐ ܠܛܘܒܢܐ
ܒܫܕܐ ܗܘ. ܘܡܢ ܚܐܪܐ ܬܘܒ ܕܠܐ ܢܦܘܩܘܢ ܥܠܘܗܝ، ܡܛܠ
ܒܢ̈ܝܗܘܢ. ܘܢܛܠܘܢܝܗ، ܥܠ ܕܫܒܩܘ ܕܐܬܐܠܨܘ ܒܕܝܢܐ ܩܫܝܐ.

58. ܗܝܕܝܢ ܓܒܪܐ ܗܘ ܡܗܝܡܢܐ ܐܡܪ ܠܗ. ܚܙܝ ܡܪܝܐ ܚܠܦ ܠܝ
ܡܠܟ ܪܒܐ. ܫܕܪ ܐܦܩ ܠܟܠܗܘܢ ܒܪ̈ܛܠܝܢܐ ܕܫܒܝܩܝܢ ܠܝ ܒܟܠ
ܕܘܟܐ: ܘܫܪܝ ܠܗܘܢ ܡܪܝܫܐ ܕܢܐܙܠ ܠܐܝܟܐ ܕܨܒܐ. ܡܪܝ، ܓܒܪ
ܦܩܕ ܠܝ ܕܐܢ ܨܒܐ ܕܒܟܢ ܢܦܩ ܠܘܬܗ. ܕܗܟܢ ܢܦܪܩܘܢܝܗ،
ܐܝܟ ܕܫܦܝܪ. ܐܢ ܨܒܐ ܕܢܐܙܠ ܒܟܢ ܢܐܙܠ ܕܠܐ ܕܚܠܐ.
ܘܐܢ ܚܙܐ ܕܢܦܘܫ ܐܚܝܕ ܠܗ ܢܬܦܪܥ ܠܗ. ܐܢ ܓܒܪ ܛܒܐ
ܡܛܠܬܐ ܡܢ ܫܒܪܗ̇ ܡܪܝܢ ܕܚܠܦ ܠܗܘܢ ܒܫܪܪܐ ܗܘܐ܀

59. ܘܗܝܕܝܢ ܦܩܕ ܥܒܕܘ ܠܚܪܘܪܐ ܕܢܩܪܘܢ ܒܟܠ ܡܕܝܢܬܐ. ܟܡ ܕܡܫܝܢ
ܐܘ ܡܗܘܐ ܠܚܕ ܡܢ ܒܪ̈ܛܠܝܢܐ. ܐܘ ܐܡܪ ܠܗܘܢ ܡܕܡ ܕܒܝܫ
ܘܫܢܝܐ. ܪܫܡ ܒܫܘܦܐ ܢܬܛܠ. ܐܠܐ ܥܠ ܐܝܟ ܢܦܫ ܘܢܫܬܒܩ
ܠܗܘܢ. ܗܝܕܝܢ ܚܕܘ ܡܗܝܡܢܐ ܕܗܘܐ ܠܗܘܢ ܡܪܝ
ܫܪ̈ܝܬܗܘܢ ܒܚܐܪܘܬܐ ܕܠܐ ܕܚܠܐ.

60. ܦܩܕ ܗܘܐ ܕܝܢ ܗܘ ܥܒܕܘ ܒܪ ܡܬܡܪܡܪ ܒܠܒܗ: ܥܠ ܕܠܐ
ܡܛܠܗ ܠܡܪܝܫܐ. ܘܡܢ ܕܫܠܛܗ ܡܛܠ ܒܐܡ̈ܬܗ ܕܡܠܟܐ ܐܚܝܢܐ
ܚܠܦ ܗܡܢܐ ܕܢܐܬܘܢ ܓܒܪ̈ܐ ܒܠܗܘܢ ܒܗ ܢܩܐ ܒܫܪ̈ܪܐ
ܘܒܠܬܚܘܡܐ ܢܗܪ̈ܐ ܘܢܐܙܠܘܢ ܡܪܝ ܛܘܒܢܐ ܒܕܡܐ ܠܦܠܛܝܢ
ܕܝܠܗ. ܘܒܟܡܐ ܩܪܐ ܐܢܘܢ ܕܢܐܟܠܘܢ ܠܚܡܐ.

61. ܗܘ ܕܝܢ ܡܪܝܫܐ ܠܐ ܨܒܐ. ܐܠܐ ܐܡܪ ܗܘܐ ܕܢܦܩ ܠܝ ܡܢ
ܡܪܝܐ ܐܠܗܐ ܕܒܡ ܓܒܪܐ ܛܘܒܢܐ ܐܟܘܠ ܠܚܡܐ.
ܐܦܝܣܗ ܕܝܢ ܡܗܝܡܢܐ ܗܘ. ܘܒܟܡܗ ܐܟܠ ܠܚܡܐ ܒܠܝܠܝܐ
ܘܓܒ̈ܝܐ ܘܗܢܐ ܡܫܝܚܐ ܕܒܟܡܗ ܡܢ ܡܪܝܐ ܢܣܒ ܗܘܐ.

62. After they had pleasantly eaten and drunk, that believer said to him, "My lord gave me instructions to tell you and urge you to come back with me, if possible, to the west, because he would like to see you; and there he will show you honour. But for the moment, I beg you, let me have a doctor brought to attend to these wounds of yours from the combs, and he will make them better. Then come with me and we will go back to the victorious emperor Constantine, where you will receive honour from him, as your labours deserve."

63. But the holy man replied, "For the sake of Christ, I abhor the restful delights of the body for I have heard said, 'Everyone who does not leave his father and his mother, his brothers and his sisters, his family and his lineage, and all that he has in the world, to take up his cross and follow me, cannot become a disciple of mine. But he who rejects his own soul for my sake shall preserve it unto eternal life' (cf. Matt 10:38–9, 19:29; Luke 14:26–7). For this reason I want to proclaim his name in this region and to turn many to him. And not in this region alone, but once I have made converts here and have built sanctuaries and monasteries for him, I will leave in them disciples of his, and I myself will come to your region and make disciples there too; and there I shall complete my course.

64. "As for your saying, 'Let me bring you a doctor,' are these lacerations worse than those earlier torments which were inflicted on my body which collapsed on the ground? But Christ, in whom I have believed, did not make me require any human assistance, but instead, after they had put vinegar, salt and asafoetida on my wounds, and it had eaten into my flesh and I was in torment, (Christ) immediately sent his angel to me in the likeness of his servant Benjamin who had baptized me, and he healed my wounds. So now too I have confidence in him that he will heal my wounds, as he did the earlier ones.

65. "But tell the believing emperor Constantine that 'Our Lord Jesus Christ in whom you have believed and have established his faith, shall preserve you and your crown, as with king David, and he will increase your fame, like Solomon's: the islands shall hear of your reputation and shall come with their gifts and do obeisance to you (cf. Ps 72:10–11; Isa 60:9); the peoples shall tremble and the nations shall fear you; and your foot shall trample upon the neck of your enemies (cf. Gen 49:8), and your right hand shall destroy your opponents. You shall be blessed and your heart shall exult in the Lord, while my spirit, and that of the many whom you

62. ܘܡܢ ܕܐܟܠܘ ܘܐܬܥܝܩܘ ܘܐܬܟܡܪܘ: ܐܡܪ ܠܗ ܡܗܝܡܢܐ ܗܘ̇.
ܡܪܝ, ܦܩܘܕ ܘܐܡܪ ܠܝ. ܕܐܡܪ ܠܟ ܘܐܦܝܣܟ: ܕܐܢ ܡܫܝܚܐ
ܒܡܢ ܬܗܘܐ ܠܡܚܙܐ ܕܒܢܝܐ ܕܢܫܝܢ. ܘܬܘܒ ܠܘܬܗ ܢܦܪܘܢ.
ܐܠܐ ܗܫܐ ܡܦܝܣ ܐܢܐ ܠܟ ܕܐܬܬܐ ܐܚܣܢܐ ܘܬܬܦܪܩ
ܠܡܫ̈ܬܘܬܐ ܗܠܝܢ ܕܩܕܡܝܟ: ܘܫܠܡ ܐܢܝܢ. ܘܬܐ ܒܡܢ ܕܢܫܡ
ܝ̈ܕܘܗܝ, ܕܡܠܟܐ ܥܒܕܐ ܡܩܛܠܢܘܗܝ. ܘܬܘܒ ܬܬܚܘܪ ܠܘܬܗ:
ܐܡܝܢܐ ܕܢܦܩ ܒܟܠܝܟ❖

63. ܗܘ ܕܝܢ ܩܕܝܫܐ ܐܡܪ ܠܗ. ܡܛܠ ܗܢܐ ܚܙܝܬ ܢܫ̈ܐ ܘܒܥܘ̈ܩܬܐ
ܦܓ̈ܪܝܟܐ ܡܛܠ ܡܫܝܚܐ. ܗܘ̇ ܕܫܡܥܬ ܕܐܡܪ. ܕܟܠ ܕܠܐ ܫܒܩ
ܠܐܒܘܗܝ, ܘܠܐܡܗ: ܘܠܐܚ̈ܘܗܝ, ܘܠܐܚܘ̈ܬܗ: ܘܠܒ̈ܢܘܗܝ
ܘܠܐܢܬܬܗ: ܘܠܟܠ ܕܐܝܬ ܠܗ ܒܥܠܡܐ: ܘܫܩܠ ܨܠܝܒܗ
ܘܐܬܐ ܒܬܪܝ. ܬܠܡܝܕܐ ܠܐ ܡܫܟܚ ܕܢܗܘܐ ܠܝ. ܘܡܢ ܕܢܘܒܕ
ܢܦܫܗ ܡܛܠܬܝ, ܢܫܟܚܝܗ ܠܚܝ̈ܐ ܕܠܥܠܡ: ܘܡܛܠ ܗܢܐ ܒܥܐ ܐܢܐ
ܕܐܚܪ ܥܡܟ ܒܐܬܪܐ ܗܢܐ. ܘܐܦܢܐ ܠܡܫܝ̈ܚܝܐ ܠܘܬܗ. ܘܠܐ
ܒܐܬܪܐ ܗܢܐ ܒܠܚܘܕ. ܐܠܐ ܡܟܐ ܕܐܬܒܪܟܬ ܗܪܟܐ. ܘܡܟܐ
ܕܒܢܝܬ ܠܗ ܡܕܒܚܐ ܘܕܝܪ̈ܬܐ. ܘܐܪܦܐ ܒܗܘܢ ܬܠܡܝܕ̈ܘܗܝ,
ܘܐܬܐ ܐܢܐ ܠܝ ܠܐܬܪܐ ܕܠܒܪ. ܘܬܘܒ ܬܗܘܐ ܐܬܠܡܕ.
ܘܬܘܒ ܐܫܠܡ ܪܘܚܝ❖

64. ܘܕܐܡܪܬ ܕܐܬܬܐ ܠܝ ܐܚܣܢܐ. ܠܡܢܐ: ܚܝ̈ܝܢ ܗܘ̈ܝܐ ܗܠܝܢ ܡܢ
ܗܠܝܢ ܕܥ̈ܒܪܐ ܘܡܬܚ̈ܠܦܐ ܕܐܬܟܡܪܘ ܦܓܪ, ܘܢܦܠ ܥܠ ܐܪܥܐ.
ܘܡܫܝܚܐ ܗܘ̇ ܕܒܗ ܗܝܡܢܬ ܠܐ ܐܫܬܒܩ ܥܠ ܐܦ̈ܝ, ܒܟܢܘܫܝܐ.
ܐܠܐ ܡܢ ܒܬܪ ܕܐܘܪܟܘ ܠܝ ܫܢ̈ܝܐ ܘܡܟܝܟܘܬܐ ܘܣܝܒܘܬܐ ܥܠ
ܡܫܝܚܘܬ, ܘܐܬܐ ܠܒܝܬ, ܘܗܘܝܬ ܒܐܘܠܨܢܐ: ܒܝܕܐ ܫܒܬܐ
ܫܕܪ ܡܠܐܟܐ ܢܝܕ: ܒܕܡܘܬܐ ܕܒܝܫܢ ܒܝܕܗ ܗܘ̇ ܕܐܡܟܕܝܢ
ܘܐܣܪ ܐܢܝܢ. ܘܐܦ ܗܫܐ ܒܠܘܗܝ, ܬܒܥܐ ܐܢܐ. ܕܗܘ ܡܟܐܒܐ
ܠܗܝ̈ ܠܣܒ̈ܪܬܐ ܗܠܝܢ. ܐܝܟ ܕܡܦܩܬܐ.

65. ܐܠܐ ܐܡܪ ܠܗ ܠܡܠܟܐ ܡܗܝܡܢܐ ܩܘܣܛܢܛܝܢܘܣ. ܕܡܪܝ̱
ܝܫܘܥ ܡܫܝܚܐ ܗܘ̇ ܕܗܝܡܢܬ ܒܗ ܘܐܘܕܝܬ ܗܝܡܢܘܬܗ: ܗܘ
ܢܛܪܟ ܘܢܬܠܟ ܐܝܟ ܕܘܝܕ ܡܠܟܐ. ܘܢܗܪ ܫܡܟ ܐܝܟ
ܫܠܝܡܘܢ. ܢܫܬܡܥ ܫܡܟ ܒܐܬܪ̈ܘܬܐ ܘܢܐܬܘܢ ܒܩܘܪ̈ܒܢܝܗܘܢ
ܘܢܣܓܕܘܢ ܠܟ. ܘܢܣܒܘܢ ܒܫܠܡܐ ܘܢܫܠܡ ܐܬ̈ܘܬܐ ܡܢܟ.
ܘܬܕܘܫ ܪ̈ܓܠܝܟ ܥܠ ܩܕܠܐ ܕܒܥܠܕܒ̈ܒܝܟ. ܘܢܣܒܘܢ ܬܫܒܘܚܬ
ܠܫܡܐܝܢ. ܘܬܗܘܐ ܒܪܝܟ ܘܢܛܪ ܠܟܝ ܒܟܪܘܒܐ. ܘܢܘܚ ܕܠܐ

have delivered from affliction, shall worship together, along with your spirit, before the tribunal of Christ. And because you have shown great concern for him and for his Church, Christ will hold you, our brother, worthy to approach to worship him, along with us, on the great day of his advent; while in this world he will not deprive your house of his benefits forever, and for you no man shall depart from his kingdom for eternal ages (cf. Gen 49: 10; 2 Chr 6:16).'"

66. Then the man knelt and did obeisance before him, and made him swear that he would give him the garment he was wearing that was full of blood from his wounds and lacerations, so that it could travel with him to the west. Only barely did he persuade him to give it to him, in exchange for another new one to put on.

67. The next day that believing man said to king Shapur, "You and all your nobles, write for me documents stating that there will be no more investigation or deceit used upon this man or on any Christian in your land." Shapur and his nobles then wrote out and sent everything which that blessed believer had asked for, showing him honour. Whereupon he sent him back to his lord amidst great honour.

68. The blessed man accompanied him as far as Edessa, where that believer urged Barse, who was the bishop in Edessa, to place the holy Gospel on the head of Mar Ma'in, and he made him a bishop. (Ma'in) then embraced and kissed that believer, saying to him, "Go in peace, and greet the victorious emperor and say to him, 'Do not be grieved because I have not come to you: I would not have been of any use to you, seeing that you are full of the faith, as I am. Instead, I have been made your associate, for you shall preach and teach in the west, and I in the east. Nevertheless, both of you shall see me in the spirit twice, and then we shall die.' Go in peace, and may the Lord be always with you."

69. So the man left and travelled to his lord. On being told everything, the emperor rejoiced, and kept a memorial on that day for all strangers and for all who had died for the sake of Christ.

70. The holy man however returned back to the mountain of Sinjar where he sold all that he possessed. Part of the proceeds he gave to the poor, while part of them he took with him. He then hired workmen, giving

ܘܕܣܦܪ̈ܝܐ ܕܐܦܣܬ ܡܢ ܐܘܠܦ̈ܢܐ ܘܪܘܚܢ ܕܠܟ: ܩܕܡ ܒܝܡ
ܕܡܫܝܚܐ ܐܚܪܢܐ ܢܫ̈ܒܚܢ. ܘܠܟ ܐܚܘܢ ܕܗܘܐ ܠܟ
ܥܘܠܠ̈ܒܢܐ ܦܓ̈ܥܐ: ܡܛܠ ܡܫܝܚܐ ܘܡܛܠ ܒܪܬܗ: ܒܟܡ
ܢܥܘܠܢ ܡܫܝܚܐ ܕܬܬܘܪܒ ܠܦܓܪܬܗ ܒܥܘܡܐ ܪܒܐ
ܕܐܬܬܗ. ܘܒܠܒܐ ܗܢܐ ܠܐ ܢܣܘܪ ܠܦܬ̈ܚܬܗ ܒܒܢܬܢ
ܠܟܠܡ. ܘܠܐ ܢܚܕ ܠܢ ܒܒܪܐ ܡܢ ܡܠܟܘܬܗ ܠܟܠܡ ܠܟܠܡܝܢ܀

66. ܗܕܝܢ ܒܪܐ ܗܘ ܒܪܢ ܘܣܓܕ ܩܕܡܘܗܝ، ܘܐܘܡܝܗ ܣܓܕ
ܕܒܬܘܬܢܐ ܗܝ ܕܠܒܝܫ ܗܘܐ ܕܠܒܠܢܐ ܗܘܬ ܕܒܟܐ ܕܡܫܝܚܘܬܗ
ܘܕܦܬܘܪܘܗܝ، ܢܬܠܘܫ ܠܗ. ܘܬܫܘܡ ܒܒܗ ܠܡܕܒܪܐ. ܘܠܡܚܣܡ ܕܝܢ
ܐܬܬܦܝܣ ܕܢܬܠܘܫ ܠܗ. ܘܫܩܠ ܕܝܢ ܗܘ ܐܣܝܪܬܐ ܚܕܬܐ
ܘܠܒܫ܀

67. ܘܒܬܪܗ ܕܗܘܒܐ ܐܡܪ ܡܗܝܡܢܐ ܗܘ ܠܥܒܘܪ ܡܠܟܐ. ܒܬܘܒ
ܠܝ ܒܬܫ̈ܒܚܬܐ ܐܢܬ ܘܒܠܗܘܢ ܪ̈ܘܪܒܢܝܟ: ܕܠܐ ܬܘܒ ܗܘܐ
ܐܦܠܡܢܐ ܐܘ ܢܒܠܐ ܠܒܪܐ ܗܢܐ. ܘܠܐ ܠܚܕ ܡܢ ܒܪ̈ܦܠܢܐ
ܒܐܬܪܢ. ܘܒܬܘܒ ܘܥܒܕ ܗܘ ܥܒܘܪ ܘܪܘܪܒܢܘܗܝ، ܒܠܡܕܡ ܐܝܟ
ܕܒܟܐ ܦܓܪܢܐ ܘܡܗܝܡܢܐ ܗܘ. ܘܦܩܕܗ ܠܡܗܝܡܢܐ ܗܘ
ܘܥܕܪܗ ܒܐܣܝܪܐ ܪܒܐ ܠܒܝܬ ܡܪܗ.

68. ܘܫܠܡ ܒܟܗ ܦܓܪܐ ܒܕܡܐ ܠܐܘܪܗܝ، ܘܐܦܝܣ ܡܗܝܡܢܐ
ܗܘ ܠܐܦܣܩܘܦܐ ܒܪܨܐ ܕܐܢܬ ܗܘܐ ܒܐܘܪܗܝ، ܘܦܩܕ ܟܠ
ܢܥܡܗ ܕܡܪܝ، ܡܟܝܢ ܐܘܢܓܠܝܘܢ ܩܕܝܫܐ: ܘܒܝܕܗ ܐܦܝܣܩܘܦܐ.
ܘܒܦܩܗ ܘܢܥܡܗ ܠܡܗܝܡܢܐ ܗܘ ܘܐܡܪ ܠܗ. ܙܠ ܒܫܠܡܐ
ܘܫܐܠ ܫܠܡܗ ܕܡܠܟܐ ܙܒܝܢܐ ܘܐܡܪ ܠܗ. ܕܠܐ ܬܬܒܝܫ ܕܠܐ
ܐܬܬ ܠܘܬܟ. ܠܟ ܡܕܡ ܠܐ ܡܘܢܐ ܗܘܬ. ܡܛܠ ܕܡܠܟܬ
ܗܘ ܡܗܝܡܢܘܬܐ ܐܒܘܗܬ، ܐܠܐ ܒܒܢ ܐܢܐ ܥܘܬܦܟ ܕܐܢܬ
ܬܟܪ ܘܬܐܠܦ ܒܡܒܪܟܐ ܘܐܢܐ ܒܡܕܢܚܐ. ܒܪܡ ܕܝܢ ܬܪܒܘܢ
ܫܡܥ ܐܢܬܘܢ ܠܝ ܒܪܘܟ: ܬܪ̈ܬܝܢ ܙܒܢܝܢ. ܘܡܢ ܡܢܟܘܢ. ܐܠܐ ܙܠ
ܒܫܠܡܐ. ܘܡܪܢܐ ܢܗܘܐ ܒܡܟܝܢ ܠܟܠܡ܀

69. ܘܦܪܫ ܒܪܐ ܗܘ ܘܫܠܡ ܠܘܬ ܡܪܗ: ܘܐܫܬܥܝ ܠܗ ܒܠܡܕܡ.
ܘܒܪ ܥܒܕ ܡܠܟܐ ܚܕ، ܘܒܒܪ ܕܗܒܪܢܐ ܒܥܘܡܐ ܗܘ ܠܟܠܗܘܢ
ܐܒܗ̈ܬܐ ܘܠܒܠ ܕܡܫܬܘ ܡܛܠ ܡܫܝܚܐ܀

70. ܡܕܝܢܐ ܕܝܢ ܒܠܦ ܘܐܙܠ ܠܦܘܪܐ ܕܫܒܛܪ. ܘܒܢ ܒܠ ܕܐܢܬ
ܗܘܐ ܠܗ. ܘܡܢܗ ܢܗܒ ܠܡܣ̈ܟܢܐ ܘܡܢܗ ܫܩܠ ܒܟܗ. ܘܗܘܐ

them a wage, and had places of prayer built, attaching monasteries, ninety six in all. And whenever he was building a monastery, he would build in it a church, whereupon he would immediately baptize some people and settle them there, leaving them as much bounty as sufficed them. He would then set off at once and start building another monastery, and when he had finished building it, with all its fittings, he set off for yet another. Such was his practice, and he built a total of ninety six monasteries, providing priests, deacons, brethren and liturgical services.

71. He converted no small number of people, and once he had confirmed them strongly in the faith of our Lord, he got up and set off, leaving them. He would travel from one town to another, proclaiming the Gospel. In this way he came as far as 'Anat, and on the banks of the Euphrates, about two miles from 'Anat, he built a small cell, where he spent seven years living a chaste life that was pleasing to God, accompanied by fasting and prayer. During this time he healed sicknesses and illnesses, and drove out demons of every sort.

72. There too he converted many people, and his fame spread through the whole of Persia. He had no one with him apart from a lion: prior to the saint's arrival there this lion had savaged and devoured a large number of people, but on coming there the holy man had forbidden it to savage or harm anyone any longer; (once) with it, he had subdued it and it lived with him for a considerable time, up to the day when he departed from this world, some twelve years, seven in the cell near 'Anat, and five in the place where he (subsequently) came and (it) was converted.

73. After he had converted many people, he heard that paganism still survived by the river Euphrates, near a town called Agrippos, having been built by king Agrippas. On learning of this, the divine man got up and rode on the lion, travelling along the banks of the Euphrates until he reached a village called Shadwa, which also had an altar of Nabu. It was

ܐܓܪ ܦܥܠܐ ܘܦܣܩ ܠܗܘܢ ܐܓܪܐ. ܘܒܢܐ ܗܘܐ ܒܝܬ ܨܠܘ̈ܬܐ ܘܕܝܪ̈ܬܐ ܥܠ ܫܡܗܘܢ ܕܬܫܥ̈ܝܢ ܘܫܡܘܢܝܬ. ܘܡܟܐ ܕܒܢܐ ܗܘܐ ܕܝܪܐ: ܒܢܐ ܗܘܐ ܒܗ ܒܝܬ ܡܫܟܢܐ. ܡܫܒܚܐ ܡܒܟܪ. ܗܘܐ ܐܢܫ̈ܐ. ܘܗܐܟܢ ܗܘܐ ܒܗ. ܘܡܬܦܪܣܐ ܗܘܐ ܠܗܘܢ ܠܒܥܘܬܐ ܒܟܠܐ ܕܣܘܦܐ ܗܘܬ ܠܗܘܢ. ܘܡܫܕܪܐ ܐܝܟ ܗܘܐ ܘܡܙܪܐ ܗܘܐ ܕܢܒܢܐ ܒܐܣܛܪܬܐ. ܘܡܟܐ ܕܒܢܗ̇ ܘܬܘܩܢܗ̇ ܘܫܟܠܠܗ̇ ܒܟܠܗܝܢ ܕܠܗ̇: ܐܝܟ ܗܘܐ ܠܐܣܛܪܬܐ ܘܗܘܒܢܐ ܗܘܐ ܒܒܪ. ܗܘܐ. ܘܗܘܐ ܒܢܐ ܬܫܥ̈ܝܢ ܘܫܡܘܢܝܬ ܕܪ̈ܝ. ܘܥܒܕ ܒܗܝܢ ܡܥ̈ܫܐ ܘܡܫܡ̈ܫܢܐ ܘܐܢܫ̈ܐ ܘܟܠܗ̇ ܬܫܡܫܬܐ.

71. ܘܐܬܠܡܕ ܒܡܟܐ ܡܫܝܚܝܐ ܕܠܐ ܒܥܘܪ. ܘܟܕ ܫܪܪ ܐܝܟܢ ܒܡܫܝܚܘܬܗ ܕܡܪܢ ܡܫܪܪܐܝܬ. ܡܢ ܝܘܡ ܘܐܝܠܦ ܐܝܟܢ: ܘܗܘܐ ܐܬܐ ܗܘܐ ܡܢ ܡܕܝܢܬܐ ܠܡܕܝܢܬܐ ܘܡܟܪܙ ܗܘܐ. ܘܐܬܐ ܒܕܡܐ ܠܒܝܬ. ܘܥܠ ܣܦܪܗ̇ ܕܦܪܬ ܥܠ ܬܪ̈ܝܢ ܡܬܚܡܝܢ ܡܢ ܒܝܬ. ܒܢܐ ܠܗ ܒܘܪܓܐ ܚܕ ܘܒܘܪܓ ܘܗܘܐ ܒܗ ܥܣܪ̈ ܫܢܝܢ. ܒܕܘܒܪ̈ܐ ܢܟܦ̈ܐ ܕܡܪܝܡ ܠܐܠܗܐ. ܒܨܘܡܐ ܘܨܠܘܬܐ. ܟܕ ܡܐܣܝܐ ܟܐ̈ܒܐ ܘܒܟܘܪ̈ܗܢܐ ܘܦܓܪ̈ ܕܝܘܐ. ܘܡܦܩ ܫܐ̈ܕܐ❖

72. ܘܐܬܠܡܕ ܬܘܒ ܬܡܢ ܒܡܟܐ ܡܫܝܚܝܐ ܘܢܩܡ ܥܡܗ ܒܟܠܗ̇ ܦܢܘ. ܐܝܟ ܕܝܢ ܠܒܝܬ ܗܘܐ ܒܥܡܗ: ܐܠܐ ܐܝܟܐ ܚܕ ܕܣܦܪܢ ܗܘܐ ܘܐܟܠ ܒܡܟܐ ܡܫܝܚܝܐ ܡܢ ܡܐܬܬܗ ܕܡܪܝܐ ܕܠܬܡܢ. ܘܡܢ ܕܐܬܐ ܗܡ ܠܗ ܬܫܡܫܬܐ ܕܠܐ ܬܘܒ ܢܣܬܘܕ ܐܘ ܢܫܒܠ ܒܢܫܐ. ܘܒܥܡܗ ܫܒܕܘܗ. ܘܗܘܐ ܒܥܡܗ ܕܒܢܐ ܠܐ ܕܒܪ. ܒܕܡܐ ܠܥܘܡܐ ܕܢܦܩ ܡܢ ܥܠܡܐ ܗܢܐ: ܐܝܟ ܫܒ̈ܝܐ ܬܬܒܣܪܐ. ܥܒܕ ܒܗܘ ܒܘܪܓܐ ܕܒܢܐ ܘܚܒܫ ܐܢܫܐ ܕܐܬܐ ܘܐܬܬܠܡܕ.

73. ܘܡܢ ܒܬܪ ܕܐܬܠܡܕ ܒܡܟܐ ܡܫܝܚܝܐ. ܥܒܕ ܕܒܥܠ ܚܦܝܬܐ ܐܝܬ ܗܘܬ ܥܠ ܦܪܬ ܢܗܪܐ. ܥܠ ܓܒ ܡܕܝܢܬܐ ܕܫܡܗ̇ ܐܓܪܦܘܣ. ܗܝ ܕܒܢܗ̇ ܗܘܐ ܐܓܪܦܘܣ ܡܠܟܐ❖ ܘܟܕ ܫܡܥ ܠܒܢܝܐ ܐܠܗܝܐ ܡܢ ܘܬܒ ܥܠ ܐܝܟܐ ܗܘ: ܘܐܬܐ ܥܠ ܣܦܪܗ̇ ܕܦܪܬ ܒܕܡܐ ܕܡܬܠܟ ܠܡܕܝܢܬܐ ܕܡܬܩܪܝܐ ܫܒܘܪܐ: ܕܐܦ ܬܡܢ ܒܠܬܐ ܐܝܬ ܗܘܬ ܕܒܗ. ܘܢܣܘܡܐ ܡܢ ܐܓܪܦܘܣ ܐܝܟ ܦܪ̈ܣܚܐ ܬܠܬܝܢ ܕܟܒܪܝܢ ܡܢܠܐ ܫܬܐ. ܘܟܕ ܒܚܪ ܒܗ̇ ܬܠܐ ܐܝܟܐ ܗܘ̇ ܢܦܫܗ ܘܫܡܥ. ܗܘ ܕܝܢ ܡܪܝܐ ܡܟܢܐ ܗܘܐ ܒܗ ܕܢܒܠܝܢ. ܘܠܐ ܐܢܫ ܡܢ ܕܟܘܬܗ. ܘܟܕ ܩܐܡ ܘܦܠܚ ܠܗ:

some two parasangs, or six miles, distant from Agrippos. As he was passing by it, the lion reared up and stopped, whereupon the holy man shouted at it to go on, but it did not budge from the spot, carrying him (still) as it stood there. The holy man then heard the sound of revelry, of singing and drums, in the village on a nearby hill where that altar stood, it being the festival of their god Nabu. Now at that time, owing to the decree of Constantine, worthy of good memory, the horn of paganism had been broken, and so out of fear for the Christians, people would hold feasts and festivals for idols in secret. Now when the holy man heard that noise he realized that it was a festival of idols, and that it was of God's doing that the lion had been checked in its path, so he said to it, "If our Lord Jesus wants us to remain here, go where he directs and bids you." Still carrying him, the lion immediately set off up the hill among all the crowd. When the people who were reclining and enjoying themselves saw this sight, everyone was frightened and terrified: they got up hastily to run away, but the blessed man stopped them and said, "Do not be afraid; I am confident in our Lord Jesus that he will turn you to him and show you his path. And if you turn to him, he will benefit you, but if you do not, then your death is before your eyes, for you cannot be sacrificing to demons and (at the same time) worship God, the Lord of all, (just) out of fear of the emperor. Rather, you should realize that it is God who assists you and delivers you from all your afflictions and disasters."

74. After he had preached to them at length, admonishing them and teaching them the law of God, some of them truly believed, while others did not believe, but out of fear of the lion they were afraid to say anything to him. It was about half an hour after they had listened to him that they believed firmly in God. The blessed man found there a cave next to the temple where they used to sacrifice to demons (which) on many occasions used to appear there. (Ma'in) went in and lived in it, building a cell outside it where he and his lion lived.

75. His reputation spread through the whole region, and every case of sickness, affliction, demonic possession, or paralysis that came to him was healed. He converted and instructed the whole area, teaching the whole of that *castra*. And when the villages round about it saw the miracles he was performing, they rejected the idols and attached themselves in love to Christ, tearing down the pagan altars from all over the country as well as from that town, as everyone believed in God.

ܫܡܥ ܩܕܝܫܐ ܩܠܐ ܕܫܘܒܚܐ ܘܕܙܡܪܐ ܘܕܛܠܝܐ ܒܗ ܒܡܥܪܬܐ
ܒܛܘܪܐ ܚܕ ܕܩܪܝܒ ܠܬܡܢ ܐܝܟܐ ܕܒܠܬܐ ܗܝ ܐܝܬ ܗܘܬ.
ܡܛܠ ܣܓܝܐܐ ܗܘ ܕܒܗ ܐܠܗܘܗܝ. ܘܒܗܘ ܕܒܢܝܐ ܡܛܠ
ܦܘܪܩܢܗ ܕܫܒܝܐ ܠܕܘܒܪܐ ܓܒܐ ܡܘܬܒܘܬܗܘܢ ܬܫܒܘܚܬܐ ܗܘܬ
ܡܪܝܐ ܕܫܦܝܘܬܐ. ܘܕܫܠܝܡ ܗܘܘ ܡܢ ܒܢܝ̈ܢܫܐ. ܘܒܫܠܡܫܬܐ
ܒܛܝܒ ܗܘܘ ܚܟܝܡܐ ܘܒܛܝܒܐ ܠܬܫܒܘܚܬܐ܀ ܘܟܕ ܫܡܥ ܩܕܝܫܐ
ܩܠܐ ܗܢܐ: ܝܕܥ ܕܚܟܝܡܐ ܐܬܘܗܝ ܕܬܫܒܘܚܬܐ. ܘܡܢ ܐܠܗܐ ܗܝ
ܕܐܬܒܠܥ ܐܪܥܐ ܗܘ ܘܐܡܪ ܠܗ. ܕܐܝܟ ܗܪܟܐ ܐܪܐ ܒܢ ܡܪܢ
ܫܡܥ ܡܫܝܚܐ ܕܢܦܫ ܠܐܒܐ ܕܬܪܝܢ ܠܟ ܘܦܩܕ ܠܟ ܕܠ.
ܘܡܚܕܐ ܒܪ ܠܓܒܝ ܠܗ ܬܪܝܢ ܘܗܠܡ ܠܛܘܪܐ ܗܘ: ܒܫܬ ܒܠܗ
ܒܥܒܐ. ܘܟܕ ܚܙܐ ܒܥܒܐ ܗܘ ܕܓܒܝܢ ܗܘܘ ܘܒܦܩܕܝܢ ܒܠ
ܚܘܐ ܗܢܐ ܒܠܝܢ ܕܚܠܘ ܘܪܒܘ: ܘܐܬܪܗܒܘ ܘܣܓܕܘ ܕܒܪܟܘܗܝ.
ܗܘ ܕܝܢ ܛܘܒܢܐ ܒܠܐ ܐܢܘܢ ܒܪ ܐܡܪ ܕܠܐ ܬܕܚܠܘܢ.
ܘܬܒܥܠ ܐܢܐ ܒܠ ܡܪܢ ܝܫܘܥ ܕܗܘ ܡܦܢܐ ܠܟܘܢ ܠܬܘܬܗ.
ܘܡܚܘܐ ܠܟܘܢ ܐܘܪܚܗ. ܐܢ ܕܝܢ ܡܬܦܢܝܢ ܐܢܬܘܢ ܠܬܘܬܗ
ܡܟܪܙ ܠܟܘܢ. ܐܠܐ ܗܐ ܡܬܘܬܒܝܢ ܩܕܡ ܒܢܝ̈ܒܘܢ. ܠܐ
ܓܝܪ ܡܫܒܚܝܢ ܐܢܬܘܢ ܕܬܗܘܘܢ ܡܕܒܚܝܢ ܠܫܐ̈ܕܐ
ܘܬܣܓܕܘܢ ܠܐܠܗܐ ܡܪܐ ܒܠ ܡܢ ܕܚܠܬܐ ܕܡܠܟܐ. ܐܠܐ
ܕܒܗ ܠܐܠܗܐ ܕܗܘ ܡܟܪܙ ܠܟܘܢ ܘܦܩܕ ܠܟܘܢ ܡܢ ܒܠܗܘܢ
ܐܘ̈ܠܨܢܝܟܘܢ ܘܒܢܝ̈ܫܬܟܘܢ.

.74 ܘܟܕ ܬܢܝ ܒܗܢ ܠܗܘܢ ܗܟܢ ܘܐܘܪܝ ܘܐܠܦ ܐܢܘܢ ܢܛܘܪܐ
ܕܐܠܗܐ. ܐܝܬ ܡܢܗܘܢ ܕܗܝܡܢܘ ܒܥܓܠܐ. ܘܐܝܬ ܡܢܗܘܢ
ܕܠܐ ܗܝܡܢܘ ܐܠܐ ܡܢ ܕܚܠܬܐ ܕܐܪܥܐ ܗܘ ܕܫܠܝܡ ܗܘܘ
ܕܢܐܡܪܘܢ ܠܗ ܡܕܡ. ܗܘܘ ܕܝܢ ܐܝܟ ܦܠܓܗ ܕܫܒܬܐ ܡܢ
ܕܐܫܬܡܥ: ܘܗܝܡܢܘ ܚܬܝܬܐܝܬ ܒܐܠܗܐ. ܘܐܫܬܥܝܘ ܠܦܘܒܝܐ
ܬܡܢ ܡܟܪܙܬܐ ܚܕܐ ܒܠ ܟܢ ܗܘ ܒܫܬ ܐܠܗ̈ܐ. ܐܝܟܢܐ
ܕܡܕܒܚܝܢ ܗܘܘ ܠܫܐ̈ܕܐ. ܘܟܠܬܐ ܗܝܟܠܐܬܐ ܐܬܚܙܝܘ ܒܗ:
ܘܒܠ ܠܗ ܘܬܡܢ ܗܘܐ، ܘܒܢܐ ܚܕ ܒܡܘܪܝܐ ܠܒܪ ܡܢܗ ܘܗܘܐ
ܒܗ: ܗܘ ܘܐܪܝܐ ܗܘ.

.75 ܘܢܦܩ ܫܡܗ ܒܒܠܗ ܗܘ ܐܬܪܐ. ܘܒܠ ܒܐܒܐ ܐܘ ܐܘܠܨܢܐ.
ܐܘ ܕܢܝܐ ܐܘ ܡܫܪܝܐ ܕܐܬܪܐ ܗܘܐ ܠܘܬܗ ܡܬܢܣܒ ܗܘܐ.
ܘܬܠܡܕ. ܘܐܠܦ ܠܒܠܗ ܗܘ ܐܬܪܐ. ܘܐܠܦ ܠܒܠܗ ܡܣܝܒܪܐ ܗܘ:
ܘܡܘܕܢܐ ܕܒܠ ܒܒܗ ܒܪ ܚܝܘ ܚܝܠܐ ܕܒܟܪ ܗܘܐ. ܘܡܫܟ

76. Now the blessed man made a pact with God that he would not leave that place in a bodily manner again during his life. However he was snatched away in the spirit twice, when he went and saw the victorious emperor and that general during the night time, occasions when they too saw him and rejoiced, along with many people from the palace who believed in God. For this they gave praise and thanks to God.

77. The blessed man was troubled in that cave by demons once he had been relieved of the trouble of paganism. The demons came upon him in all sorts of shapes and guises, in every kind of variation. The first time they came upon him was in the form and likeness of king Shapur coming along riding on a horse, whereupon, he said, a tribunal was set up and he took his seat; he then sent for him, to have him brought to his presence to frighten him. And behind Shapur there came a Marzban who belonged to king Shapur's entourage, who said to him, "Tell me, you rebel, why have you torn down these altars which were here? And why aren't you sacrificing to the gods? For the king has sent for you to interrogate you about your rebellious actions, actions by which you have been deceiving the whole world, towns and villages alike. Now the king wants you because he is preparing to impose terrible tortures on you, so sacrifice instead, and escape them. Do not allow your old age to go down in sorrow to Sheol (Gen 42:38). If, however, you are unwilling to sacrifice, just say the words 'Zeus is great,' and I will let you go. Otherwise I will bring you to the king."

78. The holy man, however, said, "I worship the Lord God who made heaven and earth, and he is Lord over all flesh." So they took him out, thrashed and stoned him, while he did not weaken from his stance. They beat him so much that his soul left his body, as he was reciting this verse, "*They surrounded me like wasps, but then were quenched like the fire from straw, and I finished them off in the name of the Lord*" (Ps117/118:12).

ܠܡܕܒܪܐ ܘܢܦܩܘ ܘܐܙܠܘ ܘܪܗܛܘ ܠܡܥܝܢܐ. ܘܥܡܪܘ ܠܒܝܬܐ
ܡܢ ܠܒܪ ܐܪܥܐ ܗܝ ܐܦ ܡܢ ܡܕܝܢܬܐ ܗܝ. ܘܗܝܡܢܘ ܠܒܪ
ܒܐܠܗܐ.

76. ܗܘ ܕܝܢ ܦܘܠܚܢܐ ܐܡܝܢ ܡܫܚܐ ܠܐܠܗܐ ܕܬܘܒ ܟܣܝܘܗܝ،
ܦܪܢܣܐܝܬ ܠܐ ܢܦܩ ܡܢ ܬܡܢ. ܐܬܚܙܝ ܕܝܢ ܪܘܚܢܐܝܬ
ܬܪܬܝܢ ܫܢܝܢ ܘܐܙܠ ܘܚܙܝܗܝ ܠܡܠܟܐ ܫܒܘܪ. ܘܠܒܪ ܫܠܝܐ ܗܘ
ܟܠܠܬܐ ܘܐܦ ܗܘ ܚܙܐܘܗܝ ܘܫܕܪܘܗ. ܘܦܪܢܣܐ ܡܢ ܟܬܪ
ܦܠܛܝܢ ܬܘܒ ܐܠܝܢ ܕܗܝܡܢܝܢ ܒܐܠܗܐ. ܘܟܠ ܗܕܐ ܥܒܕܘ
ܘܐܘܕܝܘ ܠܐܠܗܐ.

77. ܘܗܘܐ ܠܗ ܫܘܒܚܐ ܠܦܘܠܚܢܐ ܡܢ ܫܪܝܪܐ ܒܡܕܒܪܬܐ ܗܘ. ܡܢ
ܒܬܪ ܕܐܬܬܢܝܚ ܡܢ ܦܘܪܥܢܐ ܕܫܘܦܪܬܐ ܘܐܬܐ ܠܘܬܗ، ܫܪܝܪܐ
ܒܕܝܢܐ ܕܝܠܗ ܕܢܬܝܠ ܬܢܢ. ܘܫܘܠܛܢܐ ܕܟܠ ܓܝܢܝܢ. ܐܬܐ
ܒܪ ܠܘܬܗ، ܒܥܒܕܬܐ ܡܕܝܢܬܐ ܒܕܝܐ ܠܡ ܘܦܘܠܚܢܐ ܐܝܟ
ܕܡܠܟܐ ܫܒܘܪ ܒܪ ܗܘܪ ܗܘܐ ܠܗ ܗܘܫܥܐ ܘܐܬܬܐ. ܘܬܘܒ
ܠܗ ܒܐܝܡܢܐ ܘܬܘܒ. ܘܫܪܪ ܠܡ ܒܬܪܗ ܐܝܟ ܕܝܬܘܢܝܗܝ،
ܡܕܡܘܗܝ، ܕܢܗܡܢܘܢܝܗܝ. ܘܐܬܬܐ ܠܡ ܒܬܪܗ ܡܪܘܒܢܐ: ܚܕ ܡܢ
ܦܘܠܚܢܗ ܕܫܒܘܪ ܡܠܟܐ ܘܐܡܪ ܠܗ. ܐܡܪ ܠܝ ܐܝܬ ܡܪܘܕܐ.
ܠܡܠܟܐ ܒܡܘܪܬ ܟܠܗܬܐ ܗܠܝܢ ܕܐܝܬ ܗܘ، ܒܕܘܒܬܐ ܗܕܐ.
ܘܠܡܠܟܐ ܠܐ ܡܕܒܚ ܐܝܬ ܠܐܠܗܐ. ܗܐ ܒܪ ܡܠܟܐ ܫܕܪ
ܒܬܪܟ ܕܢܬܒܥ ܡܢܟ ܬܘܒܬܐ ܕܟܦܪܬ ܡܪܕܐ: ܗܠܝܢ
ܕܡܠܟܐ ܗܘܝܬ ܒܗܘܢ ܠܡܠܟܐ ܒܠܗ ܕܡܕܝܢܬܐ ܘܕܡܘܪܐ.
ܐܠܐ ܗܫܐ ܒܥܐ ܠܟ ܕܫܕܪܐ ܡܪܝܐ ܡܠܟܐ ܕܢܬܐ ܒܠܘܟ.
ܐܠܐ ܕܒܥܐ ܘܐܗܘܐ ܘܠܐ ܬܬܥܒܕ ܗܡܝܡܢܘܬܟ ܒܕܘܡܝܐ ܠܫܡܠ.
ܐܡܝܢ ܠܐ ܒܥܐ ܐܢܬ ܕܬܕܒܚ ܐܡܪ ܒܗ ܡܠܟܐ ܕܪܒ ܗܘ
ܩܘܠ. ܘܦܩܪܐ ܐܢܐ ܠܟ. ܘܐܙܠܬ ܡܢܟܠ ܐܢܐ ܠܐ ܠܟ ܠܘܬ
ܡܠܟܐ.

78. ܗܘ ܕܝܢ ܡܕܝܫܐ ܐܡܪ. ܠܡܪܝܐ ܐܠܗܐ ܦܩܕ ܐܢܐ: ܗܘ ܕܒܟܠ
ܥܕܢܐ ܘܐܪܒܐ. ܘܐܬܘܬܗ، ܡܪܝܐ ܟܠ ܟܠ ܒܢܝ. ܘܐܦܩܘܗܝ،
ܘܓܪܗ، ܘܪ ܓܒܘܗ، ܘܗܘ ܡܢ ܫܪܪܗ ܠܐ ܐܬܦܪܩ. ܡܫܐܘܗܝ،
ܡܫܘܬܐ ܦܪܢܣܝܬܐ ܒܕܘܟܐ ܕܢܦܫܗ ܡܢ ܦܓܪܗ ܢܦܩܬ.
ܘܦܩܬ ܓܒܪܐ ܗܘܢܐ ܐܡܪ ܗܘܐ. ܣܕܘܪܝܢ ܐܝܟ ܕܡܘܪܐ ܘܕܒܪܘ
ܐܝܟ ܢܘܪܐ ܕܓܠܠܐ. ܘܒܫܒܩܗ ܕܡܪܝܐ ܐܫܩܦܬ ܐܢܝ ✤

79. Then a voice came from heaven, saying, "Be of good cheer, blessed man, and gird you loins valiantly; be strengthened by the power of prayer, for the Lord is with you: the battle which is coming upon you from the Evil One is all the more cruel than the battle with the tyrant Shapur. But do not let him deceive and ensnare you in his cunning." This is what it said, and then (the voice) was silent, and Satan withdrew from him. He revived a little and got up and entered the cave, not ceasing from prayer and supplication the entire night and day.

80. Now the lion used to go out hunting each night and get what it needed for food in the way of wild animals of the steppe, but no sheep, or oxen, or cattle, or domestic animal, or human being did it approach, only gazelles, wild asses, hares, hart and other wild animals of the steppe. And if it happened that a wolf or a boar or some other harmful animal was attacking sheep or human beings, it would go out and kill the beasts and deliver what they were wanting to savage. During the day it would come and keep the blessed man company in all that he did, like a disciple with a teacher of truth.

81. On another occasion the demons came and took their stand, carrying swords and staves, as though threatening to come and kill him. But he did not stir from his position, but instead he signed himself with the sign of the holy Cross and said, "*In my affliction I called out to the Lord, and the Lord answered me and delivered my soul*" (Ps 119/120:1). Whereupon they immediately started to shriek out all over the hillside, "Fie on you, Ma'in, why have you come to drive us away from our country and our encampment where you have taken up residence? Alas for us, what has befallen us, for it seems that we are vanquished by you as well as by your companions, being made into a laughing stock all over the created world, seeing that your master Jesus has conquered our general, sending (him) with the swine into the sea (Matt 8:32). And here we are driven out by you from our encampment before the time of our end."

82. The blessed man, however, said nothing to them. Instead he fixed his gaze on heaven, and prayed to his Lord with a groan. Then his Lord, who saw his endurance, gave him the crown of victory. The Evil One

79. ܘܠܐ ܕܝܢ ܐܬܬܐ ܠܗ ܡܢ ܫܡܝܐ ܕܐܡܪ. ܐܬܠܒܒ ܕܝܢ ܛܘܒܢܐ
ܘܐܥܒܪ ܫܢ̈ܝܢ ܒܒܪܝܐܝܬ. ܘܐܬܚܝܠ ܒܫܠܝܐ ܕܛܠܝܘܬܐ.
ܕܗܘܐ ܡܪܢܐ ܒܚܝܘܗܝ ܗܘ. ܘܫܡܐ ܒܬܪ ܩܪܒܐ ܕܐܬܐ ܒܠܥܕܘܗܝ
ܛܠܝܪ ܡܢ ܒܫܡܐ. ܘܛܠܝܪ ܡܢ ܩܪܒܗ ܕܦܪܘܩܐ ܫܒܩܪ. ܐܠܐ ܠܐ
ܢܬܒܥܢ ܘܢܬܕܘܢ ܒܢܝܫܡܬܗ. ܗܠܝܢ ܐܡܪ ܗܘܐ ܘܫܠܡ.
ܘܗܦܟܐ ܐܪܝܣ ܠܗ ܡܢܗ ܘܐܬܚܝܠ ܘܠܥܠ ܘܩܡ ܒܠ ܠܗܪ؛
ܡܪܬܐ. ܘܠܐ ܫܠܐ ܡܢ ܝ̈ܠܘܬܐ ܘܡܢ ܒܪܘܬܐ ܠܠܝܐ ܒܠܗ
ܘܐܝܡܡܐ.

80. ܐܪܥܐ ܕܝܢ ܗܿܘ ܢܦܩ ܗܘܐ ܠܡܕܢܚܐ ܒܠ ܠܠܝܐ. ܘܫܦܠ ܗܘܐ
ܡܣܟܢ ܡܟܒܠܘܬܗ ܡܢ ܫܦܘܬܐ ܕܕܒܪܐ. ܠܒܢܐ ܕܝܢ ܐܘ
ܠܬܘܪܐ ܐܘ ܠܒܝܬܐ ܐܘ ܠܫܦܘܬܐ ܕܒܥܐ ܠܗ ܦܪܒ ܗܘܐ.
ܘܠܐ ܠܒܢ̈ܝܫܐ. ܐܠܐ ܠܦܬܟܐ ܘܠܒܕ̈ܪܐ ܘܠܐܕ̈ܪܒܐ ܘܐܝܟ
ܠܐܬܪܐ ܘܠܥܪܒܐ ܕܫܦܘܬܐ ܕܕܒܪܐ. ܘܐܝܟ ܒܪܫܐ ܗܘܬ ܐܘ
ܕܐܡܒܐ ܘܚܘܪܐ ܘܡܢ ܫܦܘܬܐ ܒܫ̈ܥܬܐ. ܘܐܬܠܡ ܗܿܘ ܒܠ
ܒܢܐ ܐܘ ܒܠ ܒܢ̈ܝܫܐ. ܐܪܠ ܗܘܐ ܘܦܠܠ ܗܘܐ ܠܗ̈ܝܡ
ܘܡܒܠܠ ܗܘܐ ܠܗܿܘ ܡܕܡ ܕܒܥܝܢ ܗܿܘ̈ ܕܢܣܒܠܝܢ܀ ܘܒܐܝܡܡܐ
ܒܠܗ ܐ̈ܬܐ ܗܘܐ ܘܡܬܠܒܢܐ ܠܗ ܠܛܘܒܢܐ ܒܒܠܒܕܡ. ܐܝܟ
ܬܠܡܝܕܐ ܠܪܒܐ ܕܒܪܪܐ܀

81. ܬܘܒ ܕܝܢ ܒܙܒܢܐ ܐܚܪܢܐ ܐܬܘ ܫܕ̈ܝܐ: ܘܩܡܘ ܘܛܒܥܘ ܗܦܘܟܐ
ܘܣܘܦܪܐ. ܘܗܘܘ ܠܗܘܢ ܐܝܟ ܒܢ̈ܝܢ ܒܠܗܘܢ. ܕܢܐܬܘܢ ܠܡ
ܢܛܠܘܢܝܗܝ. ܗܘ ܕܝܢ ܡܢ ܕܡܒܬܗ ܠܐ ܐܪܝܣ. ܐܠܐ ܣܠܩ
ܢܦܫܗ ܒܛܘܦܣܐ ܕܝ̈ܠܕܬܐ ܡܕܝܢܐ ܘܐܡܪ. ܠܡܪܝܐ ܒܐܘܠܨܢܝ
ܩܪܝܬ: ܘܫܡܥ ܡܪܝܐ ܘܦܨܢ̈ܝ ܠܢܦܫܝ. ܘܡܚܕܐ ܗܘܘ ܡܛܠܠܝܢ
ܒܟܠܗ ܗܿܘ ܛܘܪܐ ܐܝܟ ܗܘܐ ܡܢܗ ܡܚܝܡ. ܠܡܪܝܐ ܐܬܝܬ ܕܬܛܪܘܕ
ܠܝ ܡܢ ܐܬܪܝ ܘܡܢ ܡܫܪܝܬܝ. ܗܘܐ ܒܪܝ ܐܝܬ ܒܗܿ. ܘܝ ܠܝ
ܡܢܐ ܗܘܐ ܠܝ. ܕܒܒܪ ܡܚܝܢ ܐܝܟ ܕܡܢ ܚܒ̈ܪܝܢ ܡܬܕܒܚܝܢ.
ܘܗܐ ܒܒܢܝܢ ܒܘܣܡܐ ܒܟܠܗ ܒܪܝܬܐ. ܕܕܒ ܚܠܘܬܝ ܐܒܘ
ܢܫܒܒ ܪܒܒܢ ܘܫܒܪ ܒܥܝܪܐ ܒܓܘ ܡܟܐ: ܘܗܐ ܚܝ ܡܒܒܘܢ
ܡܢ ܡܫܪܝܬܢ ܡܬܦܪܕܝܢ. ܒܕ ܗܿܘܐ ܕܒܢܐ ܕܫܠܡܢ.

82. ܗܘ ܕܝܢ ܛܘܒܢܐ ܡܕܡ ܠܐ ܐܡܪ ܠܗܘܢ. ܐܠܐ ܚܪܪ ܠܫܡܝܐ
ܬܠܐ ܗܘܐ ܘܠܒܪܗ ܒܫܝܓܘܬܐ ܡܝܠܐ ܗܘܐ܀ ܘܡܢܗ ܕܢܚܐ

fought with him in all sorts of varied shapes, looking like wanton camels, poisonous snakes and serpents, all sorts of fierce animals, or beautiful women or strong men. None, however, managed to harm him, but instead they retreated in shame, vanquished by the power of his prayer.

83. All this, and more, did Christ perform at the hand of his servant, Mar Ma'in: the Evil One was vanquished, the holy man was resplendent, and God was praised. For human tongue is insufficient to relate how many sicknesses and illnesses God visited at the hand of his athlete, and to how many people he granted healing through his prayers, and how many he turned away from error to God.

84. As for the ninety six monasteries that he built on mount Sinjar, our Lord granted that they became great and renowned in his own days.

85. After all these wonders that God performed at his hand, his Lord wished to take him to himself. (Ma'in) realised in his own soul that he was about to depart from this world, so he sent for and brought the surrounding villagers and said to them, "Let us keep vigil and perform the (Eucharistic) Offering and the Office, and pray together to God, for I am about to depart from this world to go to our Lord Jesus Christ." So they kept vigil, and performed the Offering, and they ate and drank, enjoying themselves in his presence.

86. On the following morning, while the whole encampment was gathered, he stood up and stretched out his hands towards heaven; as he raised his gaze to the heights, he addressed God in a loud voice, "Lord Most High, Father and Sender of our Lord Jesus Christ who came to deliver the world from error into knowledge of truth, hear, Lord, the prayer of your servant who calls upon you at this moment; act mercifully and with compassion towards my sinful soul, also when you come to dissolve heaven and earth, to give a blessed state to the just and torment and darkness to the wicked. In my case, someone who has sinned against you and stretched out my hands to shed the blood of your servants when I did not (yet) know you: behold, I have endured sufferings, beatings and lacerations for your name's sake; I have not denied you. While I

ܡܫܒܪܢܘܬܗ ܢܣܒ ܠܗ ܒܠܒܐ ܕܪܒܘܬܐ. ܘܟܕ ܐܡܪ ܒܗܘ
ܒܢܫܐ ܒܟܠ ܐܣܟܡܝܗܘܢ ܘܒܟܠ ܦܘܠܚܝܗܘܢ: ܒܪܒܘܬ ܓܒܠܐ
ܒܗܪܝ ܘܒܪܒܘܬ ܐܟܪܝܐ ܒܢܫܐ ܘܢܨܚܢܐ ܘܒܪܒܘܬܐ ܕܟܠ
ܢܫܘܗܝ ܒܢܫܬܐ: ܘܒܪܒܘܬܐ ܕܢܫܐ ܥܢܝܬܐ: ܘܒܪܒܘܬܐ
ܕܐܢܫܐ ܣܓܝܐܬܐ. ܘܠܐ ܐܫܟܚܘ ܐܣܛܘܪܗܘܢ ܕܝܢ: ܘܒܗܘܬܘ
ܘܡܢܝܢ ܕܐܙܕܒܢܘ ܡܢ ܚܝܠܐ ܕܨܠܘܬܗ❖

83. ܗܠܝܢ ܕܝܢ ܘܕܡܝ̈ܢܐ ܡܢ ܗܠܝܢ ܣܓܝ ܡܥܒܕܐ ܒܐܝܕܐ ܕܥܒܕܗ
ܡܪܝ ܡܥܝܢ. ܘܒܢܫܐ ܐܙܕܒܢ ܘܡܕܝܢܬܐ ܐܬܚܙܝ ܘܐܠܗܐ
ܐܫܬܒܚ. ܠܐ ܓܝܪ ܗܘܐ ܦܘܡܐ ܕܒܢܝ̈ܢܫܐ ܕܢܐܡܪ ܕܟܡܐ
ܟܕ̈ܟܐ ܘܒܡܪ̈ܗܘܢܐ ܗܦܟ ܐܠܗܐ ܒܐܝܕܐ ܕܐܬܠܛܫܗ. ܘܠܒܟܡܐ
ܒܢ̈ܫܐ ܢܣܒ ܫܘܠܛܢܐ ܒܝܕ ܨܠܘܬܗ. ܘܒܟܡܐ ܒܢ̈ܫܐ ܐܦܩ
ܡܢ ܦܓܪܝܗܘܢ ܠܘܬ ܐܠܗܐ.

84. ܒܗܘܪܐ ܕܝܢ ܗܠܝܢ ܬܫ̈ܒܚܢ ܘܫܬܐ ܕܒܢܐ ܒܦܘܪܐ ܕܡܫܝܚ.
ܒܫܘ̈ܚܬܗ ܢܣܒ ܡܪܝ ܘܗܘܘ ܒܗܘܪܐ ܙܘܪܐ ܘܡܫܒ̈ܚܗܐ.

85. ܘܡܢ ܒܬܪ ܗܠܝܢ ܟܠܗܝܢ ܬܕܡܪ̈ܬܐ ܕܣܥܪ ܐܠܗܐ ܒܐܝܕܗ.
ܝܗܒ ܡܪܗ ܕܢܦܩܘܗ ܠܘܬܗ. ܘܝܗܒ ܠܗ ܒܢܦܫܗ ܕܢܦܩ ܠܗ ܡܢ
ܒܠܡܐ ܗܢܐ❖ ܘܫܕܪ ܐܝܟ ܠܡܘܪܐ ܕܫܒܘܪܗܘܢ، ܘܐܡܪ ܠܗܘܢ.
ܢܟܢ ܫܘܪܐ ܘܦܘܪܢܐ ܘܬܫܡܫܬܐ ܘܢܝܠܐ ܠܐܠܗܐ
ܐܒܘܢܐ. ܕܐܢܐ ܡܒܠ ܢܦܩ ܐܢܐ ܠܝ ܡܢ ܒܠܡܐ ܗܢܐ. ܠܘܬ
ܡܪܝ ܢܣܒ ܡܫܝܚܐ. ܘܒܟܕ ܫܘܪܐ ܘܦܘܪܢܐ ܘܐܟܠܘ
ܘܐܫܬܝܘ ܘܒܣܡܘ ܒܡܘܗܒܬܗ.

86. ܘܡܢ ܦܢܐ ܐܚܪܢܐ ܗܘ ܟܕ ܒܢܫܐ ܒܠܗ ܡܕܝܢܬܐ: ܘܫܦܠ
ܐܒܘܗܝ، ܠܡܫܝܚܐ ܘܬܠܬܐ ܚܝܪܗ ܠܒܪܘܟܐ: ܘܒܡܠܐ ܪܒܐ ܐܡܪ
ܗܘܐ ܠܘܬ ܐܠܗܐ. ܡܪܝܐ ܡܪܝܡܐ ܐܒܘܗܝ، ܘܡܠܟܗ ܕܡܪܝ
ܢܣܒ ܡܫܝܚܐ: ܕܐܬܐ ܕܢܦܘܩ ܒܠܡܐ ܡܢ ܦܓܪܬܐ
ܠܕܒܬܐ ܕܙܕܝܩܐ: ܥܒܕ ܡܪܝ ܨܠܘܬܗ ܕܒܒܝܬܢ ܕܦܢܐ ܠܝ
ܒܒܥܬܐ ܗܕܐ. ܘܒܟܕ ܬܫܒܘܚܐ ܘܣܓܕܐ ܟܠ ܢܦܫ ܣܠܩܬܐ.
ܘܡܢܐ ܕܐܬܬܐ ܐܝܟ ܕܬܫܪܐ ܫܒܝܐ ܘܐܪܒܥܐ: ܘܬܬܠ ܠܦܓܪܐ
ܠܕܝܢܐ ܘܫܘܢܝܐ ܘܫܒܘܩܐ ܠܚܛ̈ܗܐ: ܘܐܢܐ ܕܫܠܛܬ ܠܝ
ܘܐܫܬܠܛܬ ܐܢܐ، ܒܪܚܡܐ ܕܒܪܝܬܝ: ܟܕ ܠܐ ܢܕܒ ܗܘܝܬ ܠܝ.
ܘܗܐ ܫܒܪܬ ܣܓܝ̈ܐ ܘܢܟܪ̈ܝܐ ܘܦܘܪܢܐ ܡܛܠ ܫܡܟ. ܘܠܐ
ܒܦܪܬ ܟܢ. ܘܕܐܬܠܝܬ ܠܒܘܪܐ ܕܒܢܦܘܪܢ ܟܢ: ܗܐ ܐܦܫܬ

forced a few to deny you, behold I have turned many back to you by means of the power which you gave me. While I tore down your shrines, behold I have erected your altars once again everywhere. Lord, remember this and have mercy on me, for I did all these things out of ignorance long ago.

87. "Give rest to the spirit of the believing emperor, and govern his household; hold me worthy to see them in your Kingdom. Exalt the horn of your Church, raise up and confirm her faith, grant her peace and welfare all the days that the world lasts. Act mercifully with sinners who call upon you, and may mercy be upon this place and upon its inhabitants; upon this village and the communities of the monasteries cause your right hand to rest. Cause to cease from their midst the sword, captivity, famine, pestilence, and all evil plagues.

88. "And may the memory of anyone who makes memory of me be before you; and may anyone who swears falsely by my name not be victorious before you. And may everyone who remembers me in faith fare well; may your grace shine out on this monastery: guide it as your mercy desires. May your benefits never be lacking from it, but rather, increase your blessings upon it. May your compassion be upon all your creation. Receive, O Lord, my spirit and give it rest in the abode of the just. And from all that you have created in heaven and on earth may praise ascend to you at all times, Father, Son and Holy Spirit, for ever, amen."

89. When he had finished his prayer and all the gathering had said "Amen," he summoned two of our brethren from the village and gave them authority over the monastery. He then reposed in peace. These brethren closed his eyes and performed his funeral rites. The entire people who were there escorted him to his burial with psalms and canticles of the Holy Spirit, burning fragrant incense before him. They laid him there in the monastery he had built. They buried him in his cloak and his tunic, because he had made them swear to do so.

90. Now the blessed man died some 114 years of age. He had entered upon instruction about Christ and had approached martyrdom when he was aged about 60, in the first year of the emperor Constantine's reign. He was imprisoned for three years after he had been instructed, because of the war which Constantine had engaged in with king Shapur, conquering

ܠܡܫܝܚܐ ܠܘܬܟ ܒܫܠܡܐ ܕܐܝܬ ܢܦܩܬ ܠܟ. ܘܕܡܘܣܦܬ ܠܡܬܒܠܥܘ: ܗܐ ܬܘܒ ܝܬܝܪܬ ܡܕܒܪܢܝܢ ܒܟܠ ܕܘܟܐ. ܡܪܝ، ܐܬܕܟܪ ܗܠܝܢ ܘܪܚܡ ܥܠܝ: ܡܛܠ ܕܕܠܐ ܒܥܕܬܐ ܦܪܫܬ ܗܠܝܢ ܡܢ ܠܘܩܕܡ.

87. ܐܚܝܕ ܪܘܚܗ ܕܡܠܟܐ ܡܗܝܡܢܐ ܘܕܒܪ ܒܝܬܗ. ܘܐܥܒܕ ܕܐܝܟܐ ܐܢܘܢ ܒܡܠܟܘܬܟ. ܘܡܦܪܣ ܡܢܗ ܕܒܝܬܟ ܘܐܦܝܣ ܘܫܪܪ ܗܝܡܢܘܬܗ. ܘܗܘܐ ܠܗ ܫܝܢܐ ܘܫܠܡܐ ܒܟܠܗܘܢ ܘܡܕܝܢܬܐ ܕܐܬܪܗ ܟܠܗ. ܘܟܠ ܫܘܠܛܢܐ ܕܦܪܣ ܠܟ ܒܝܕ ܐܝܕܝܐ. ܘܟܠ ܐܬܪܐ ܗܢܐ ܘܟܠ ܡܕܝܢܬܗ، ܢܦܩܘ ܐܝܕܝܐ. ܘܟܠ ܡܠܬܐ ܗܕܐ ܘܒܡܕܝܢܬܐ ܕܕܝܪ̈ܬܐ ܐܝܟ ܡܥܝܢ. ܘܡܛܠ ܡܢ ܒܗܘ̈ܢ ܚܪܒܐ ܘܫܒܝܐ ܘܟܦܢܐ ܘܡܘܬܢܐ: ܘܟܠܗܘܢ ܡܫܝܚܝܐ ܒܫܝܢܐ.

88. ܘܟܠ ܕܒܥܐ ܠܟ ܕܡܪܢܐ ܢܗܘܐ ܕܡܪܢܗ ܡܕܡܝܢ. ܘܟܠ ܕܢܐܡܐ ܒܫܡܟ ܒܪ ܟܠܘܬܟ ܠܐ ܢܒܥܐ ܡܕܡܝܢ. ܘܟܠ ܕܢܬܕܒܪܘܢ ܒܡܗܝܡܢܘܬܐ ܢܗܘܐ ܠܗ ܕܫܦܝܪ. ܘܟܠ ܒܡܕܝܢܐ ܗܢܐ ܬܕܝܪ ܠܨܒܘܬܟ. ܘܕܒܪܢܗ، ܐܝܟ ܕܡܚܝܢ ܐܢܫ̈ܝܢ. ܘܠܐ ܢܫܬܪܘܢ ܒܗ ܠܨ̈ܠܘܬܟ. ܐܠܐ ܐܬܚܙܝܐ ܒܗ ܒܡܪܘܬܟ. ܘܟܠ ܟܠܗ ܒܪܝܬܟ ܬܗܘܐ ܡܪܚܡܢܘܬܟ. ܘܡܟܠ ܡܪܝ، ܪܘܚܝ ܘܐܢܫܝܢܘܬܗ̇ ܒܡܥܒܕܢܐ ܕܕܝܢܐ. ܘܡܢ ܟܠ ܕܒܪܝܬ ܒܫܡܝܐ ܘܒܐܪܥܐ ܥܒܕܢܐ ܢܗܘ ܠܝ ܒܥܠܡ: ܐܒܐ ܘܒܪܐ ܘܪܘܚܐ ܩܕܝܫܐ ܠܥܠܡܝܢ ܐܡܝܢ.

89. ܘܒܪ ܫܠܡ ܨܠܘܬܗ ܘܐܡܪ ܟܠܗ ܟܢܘܫܝܐ ܗܘ̇ ܐܡܝܢ. ܡܪܐ ܠܬܪ̈ܝܢ ܡܢ ܐܚ̈ܝܢ ܕܡܕܝܢܬܐ ܘܦܩܕ ܐܢܘܢ ܟܠ ܒܡܕܝܢܬܐ ܘܫܒܚ ܒܥܠܡܐ. ܘܗܠܝܢ ܐܚ̈ܐ ܒܚܘܒܗ، ܘܒܫܝܢܗ، ܘܟܠܗ ܒܝܬܐ ܕܐܝܬ ܗܘܐ ܬܡܢ ܒܫܝܢܗ، ܘܒܪܘܚܗ، ܒܡܕܝܢܬܐ: ܘܒܬܫܒܘܚܬܐ ܕܪܘܚܐ ܩܕܝܫܐ. ܒܪ ܡܙܡܪܝܢ ܗܘܠܠܐ ܘܬܫܒ̈ܚܬܐ ܩܕܡܘܗܝ، ܘܩܒܪܘܗܝ، ܬܡܢ ܒܡܕܡܪܐ ܕܒܟܐ. ܡܝܬܘܗܝ، ܕܝܢ ܒܟܠܗ ܘܒܡܘܬܗ ܡܛܠ ܕܗܒܝܐ ܐܘܟܝ ܐܝܘ ❖

90. ܡܢܬ ܕܝܢ ܠܦܘܢܐ ܐܝܟ ܒܪ ܡܐܐ ܘܐܪܒܥܬܥܣܪܐ ܫܢܝܢ. ܟܠ ܕܝܢ ܠܬܠܡܝܕܘܗܝ ܕܫܡܥܘܢܐ ܘܐܬܦܪܫ ܠܣܗܕܘܬܐ ܐܝܟ ܒܪ ܬܠܬܝܢ ܫܢܝܢ. ܗܘܬ ܣܗܕܘܬܗ ܒܫܢܬܐ ܕܡܠܟܘܬܐ ܕܐܡܠܟܝ ܘܡܘܪܝܩܝܘܣ ܡܠܟܐ. ܘܗܘܐ ܚܝܐ ܬܠܬ ܫܢܝܢ ܡܢ ܒܬܪ ܕܐܬܬܠܝܕ. ܡܛܠ ܡܪܝܐ ܕܟܠܗ ܕܡܘܪܝܩܝܘܣ. ܒܪ ܡܫܟܐ

and subduing him in the victory which God gave him. In the third year, when (Shapur) was free from war, he passed sentence on the holy man, and the believer, who had come to receive tribute from Shapur and to grant him peace, saw him and went back and told the emperor, then returning to deliver him.

91. He resided 37 years in the mountain of Sinjar, building monasteries. He was seven years in the cell at 'Anat by the Euphrates, and six years in the mountain, in the village Shadbo. He completed his days with a good reputation. May his memory be for a blessing, and his prayer, along with that of all the saints his companions, assist us in both worlds, amen.

Ended is the history of the holy Mar Ma'in, and of the Persian saints, his companions. Through their prayers and supplications may our Lord grant peace and welfare among his people and in his Church, and in the four quarters (of the world) until the end of the world, amen.

ܗܘܐ ܒܗ ܫܒܘܪ ܡܠܟܐ. ܘܪܚܡܗܝ ܘܫܒܚܗܝ ܒܝܘܡܬܐ ܕܝܗܒ ܠܗ ܐܠܗܐ. ܘܒܫܢܬܐ ܬܠܬܬܐ ܗܘ ܒܛܠ ܡܢ ܩܪܒܐ: ܕܝܗ ܠܡܪܝܐ. ܘܣܝܡܗܝ ܡܗܝܡܢܐ ܗܘ ܕܝܗܒ ܗܘܐ ܕܢܗܒ ܡܚܝܠ ܡܕܬܐ ܘܫܩܠ ܠܗ ܫܝܢܐ. ܘܫܠܡ ܘܐܡܪ ܠܡܠܟܐ ܘܢܣܒ ܘܦܪܩܗ.

91. ܘܡܢ ܬܡܢ ܘܫܒܥ ܫܢܝܢ ܒܦܘܠܚܢܐ ܕܫܝܢܐ. ܒܗ ܚܢܐ ܕܡܪ̈ܬܐ. ܘܫܒܥ ܫܢܝܢ ܒܒܘܪܟܐ ܕܚܝܬ ܥܠ ܓܒܝ ܦܪܬ. ܘܫܒܥ ܫܢܝܢ ܒܦܘܪܢܐ ܕܫܒܥ ܡܪܬܐ. ܘܫܠܡ ܢܘܚܬܗ ܒܫܡܝܐ ܫܦܝܪܐ܀ ܕܘܒܪܗ ܠܒܘܪܟܬܐ ܘܡܠܘܬܗ ܥܡ ܕܒܠܗܘܢ ܩܕ̈ܝܫܐ ܒܢܘ̈ܬܗ ܬܒܪܟ ܠܝ ܒܨܠܘ̈ܬܗܘܢ ܠܥܠܡܐ ܐܡܝܢ.

ܫܠܡܬ ܬܫܒܘܚܬܐ ܕܩܕܝܫܐ ܡܪܝ ܡܥܝܢ: ܐܦ ܕܩܕ̈ܝܫܐ ܒܢܘ̈ܬܗ:
ܗܢܝܢ ܦܪܘܩܐ ܕܥܠܝ̈ܬܗܘܢ ܘܒܬܟܫ̈ܦܬܗܘܢ ܢܛܠ ܡܪܢ
ܫܝܢܐ ܘܫܠܡܐ ܒܥܠܡܗ ܘܒܕܬܗ ܟܐܒܪ̈ܐ ܦܫܝܬܐ ܒܕܡܐ
ܠܫܘܠܡܗ ܕܥܠܡܐ ܐܡܝܢ.

ANNOTATION

Title Ma'in: the vocalization is uncertain; see Hoffmann 28, who opts for Mu'ain (followed by BHO 783), whereas Fiey preferred Ma'in, and this is followed here.

2 mighty athlete (*atliṭa ḥliṣa*): the combination is probably deliberately based on 4 Maccabees 6:10. The term "athlete" features again in **82**, and is to be found in several of the Shapur Martyr Acts, e.g. *AMS* II, 316 (Barhadbeshabba), 390 (Aqebshma); IV, 140 (Jacob and Azad).

3 Sinjar in Persian territory: Sinjar (Singara) was ceded to the Persians in 363.

educated in literature and in the Magian religion: two different topics are probably implied: compare the *History of Sulṭan Mahdukt*, where the three children of the Zoroastrian kinglet Pawlar "were educated in secular literature (*b-sepre 'almanaye*) and especially in the babbling of the Magian religion" (*AMS* II, 4). Whereas the former involved reading and writing (thus Aba [ed. Bedjan *Histoire de Mar Jabalaha...*, 210] was educated in *sepra parsaya*), the latter implied learning by rote, involving the *reṭna da-mgushe*, "the murmuring of the Magians", referred to in Pethion (*AMS* II, 561), on which see J. Greenfield, "RTYN MGWŠ," in *Joshua Finkel Festschrift* (New York, 1974), 63–9.

4 the so-called Nazarene: Mt. 2:23 etc. See also the annotation to **39**.

resuscitated himself (*naḥḥem hu leh*): this unusual phrase is very probably a good indication of a sixth-century date, for active forms, such as this, were often preferred by miaphysite authors, instead of the traditional passive, *etnaḥḥam*.

6 deserted town called Dura: likewise **43**. The description will refer to Dura Europos.[17] The term "deserted" rules out Fiey's suggestion (p. 450) that *dwr'* is an error for *dr'* Dara, founded by Anastasius in 508; Fiey then went on to use 508 as a *terminus post quem* for dating the *History of Ma'in*: although this cannot be taken as valid evidence, a sixth-century date does indeed seem likely (see Introduction).

"mourner" (*abila*): the term is quite commonly used of ascetics unattached to monasteries.

Benjamin: not otherwise known.

7 Doda: the statement that he was skinned alive provides a strong case for identifying him with the Dado of *AMS* IV, 218–9 (the beginning of this is unfortunately lost); Fiey 443 also opts for this identification. The only other martyr under Shapur who suffered in this horrific way was Ma'ne (*AMS* II, 55). The paragraph rather awkwardly separates **6** and **8**, which may suggest that it is a secondary addition.

10 baptismal mark of salvation (*rushma d-ḥayye*): *rushma* is regularly used in the context of baptism, and *rushma d-ma'mudita* features in several Martyr Acts; the phrase used here, however, is not so commonly found, and the only other example of it in the Persian Martyr Acts is *AMS* IV, 161 (Gubralaha and Qazo); it features elsewhere, for example, in the Acts of John (ed. W. Wright; London, 1871), 1:53 and the Syrian Orthodox Rite of Monastic Profession.

11–28 Only here among the Shapur Martyr Acts is a lengthy catechetical passage to be found. A more extended passage of this sort is to be found in the Armenian *Teaching of St Gregory*, part of the *History of Agat'angelos*. See the annotated English translation in R. W. Thomson, *The Teaching of St Gregory* (Cambridge Mass. 1970; new edition Crestwood NY, 2001); there are, however, no links between the two texts. In many respects the phraseology used in these sections is fairly archaic.

11 Child (*yalda*): the term, added in the margin in the manuscript, is frequently used by Syriac writers alongside "Son".

Let us make: this was a key passage (along with Gen. 11:7 ("Let us confuse...") in Christian exegetical tradition: whereas (for example)

[17] This was assumed by F. Cumont, *Fouilles de Doura-Europos (1922–3)* (Paris, 1926), lxviii, among the list of "Témoignages des écrivains anciens sur Doura-Europos."

Philo had taken the plural as referring to the angels, along with God, Christian writers from the second century AD onwards assumed that God the Father was addressing the Son or both the Son and the Holy Spirit (as here); the former interpretation, already found in Justin Martyr, features in Ephrem (*Commentary on Genesis* I.23, *Hymns on Faith* 6), whereas the latter first occurs in Irenaeus and was taken up by both Basil of Caesarea and Gregory of Nyssa (for references, see M. Alexandre, *Le commencement du livre Genèse I–V* [Christianisme Antique 3; Paris, 1988], 169–73); a reference to the Trinity is also seen in several Syriac authors, notably Narsai (*Homélies sur la Création,* ed. Ph. Gignoux, Patrologia Orientalis 34:3–4, 1968), III, lines 245–59, and Jacob of Serugh (*Homélies contre les Juifs*, ed. M. Albert, Patrologia Orientalis 38:1, 1976), I, lines 131–40).

17 consubstantial (*bar kyana*): this represents older terminology (as opposed to the innovations of the sixth century, such as *bar ituta*, *shawe-b'usya*).

entered her womb through the hearing of her ears: the imagery of Mary's conception through her ear (i.e. hearing and consenting to Gabriel's message) is widespread in early Syriac literature (and can be found in some Greek and Latin texts as well): it provides a typological contrast with Eve's unthinking listening to the serpent. See, for example, Ephrem, *Hymns on Virginity* 23:5, "Mary conceived our Lord as a result of (lit. from) her hearing." The typological contrast with Eve is very commonly brought out, as Ephrem, *Hymns on the Church* 49:7, "Just as death entered and was poured out from the small womb of that ear (sc. of Eve), so through a new ear Life entered and was poured out from Mary" (the *Commentary on the Diatessaron* 20:32, available here only in Armenian, is very similar); *Nachträge zu Ephrem Syrus* (ed. E. Beck; CSCO 364, Scr. Syri 159; 1975), *Sermo* II, lines 161–6, "By means of the serpent the Evil One/ poured poison into the ear of Eve;/ the Good One brought down His mercy,/ and entered through Mary's ear:/ through the gate by which Death entered/ Life also entered, putting Death to death." For examples in Greek, see N. Constas, *Proclus of Constantinople and the cult of the Virgin in Late Antiquity* (Supplements to Vigiliae Christianae 66; Leiden, 2003), 273–313; in Latin, see for example Zeno of Verona (Corpus Christianorum, Series Latinus XXII), *Tractatus* I.3.19: "quia suasione per aurem inrepens diabolus Euam vulnerans interemerat, per aurem intrat Christus in Mariam." For the idea as expressed in early Christian art, see K. Urbaniak-Walczak, *Die "Conceptio per aurem". Untersuchungen zum Marienbild in Ägypten unter besonderer Berücksichtigung der*

Malereien in el-Bagawat (Arbeiten zum spätantieken und koptischen Ägypten 2; Altenberge, 1992).

18 releasing him from the bond: this reflects the identification of Simeon the Old Man as Simeon bar Sira, with his father's name being taken as *asira*, "bound", rather than as Sira. For this Syriac exegetical tradition, see J. F. Coakley, "The Old Man Simeon (Luke 2:25) in Syriac tradition," *Orientalia Christiana Periodica* 47 (1981): 189–212.

until (*'ad*): the manuscript has *kad*, which would require a translation "once he had come"; this is possible, but *kad* would be an easy graphic misreading/corruption of *'ad*.

22 he had put on a body (*pagra lbesh*): this is the standard phrase to denote the incarnation, found regularly in early Syriac texts, continuing in use later alongside more precise equivalents of Greek *esarkōthē* (*etgashsham*, *etbassar*); see in general S. P. Brock, "Clothing metaphors as a means of theological expression in Syriac tradition," in *Typus, Symbol, Allegorie bei den östlichen Vätern und ihren Parallelen im Mittelalter*, ed. M. Schmidt (Regensburg, 1982), 11–38, repr. in *Studies in Syriac Christianity* (Aldershot, 1992), ch. XI.

23 El, El: whereas the Greek has "Eli, Eli," "My God, my God", the form without the suffix "my," as here, is following the Peshitta at Matt 27:46.

24 "Take, eat, …": the slight alterations from the biblical text will probably be due to the influence of one of the liturgical forms of the Institution Narrative in the numerous Syriac anaphoras. A large bilingual (Syriac-English) collection of Syrian Orthodox Anaphoras can be found in Athanasius Y. Samuel, *Anaphoras. The Book of the Divine Liturgies* (Lodi NJ, 1991).

26 will I too deny: instead of the future *ekpor* of the Old Syriac and Peshitta Gospel text, the participle (denoting a more imminent future) is used here, with the pronoun "I" reduplicated for emphasis.

30 Barse: bishop of Edessa 371–73 (when he was exiled; he died in 378); previously he had been bishop of Harran. He is mentioned in the *Chronicle of Edessa* (under the Seleucid years 672 and 689), and Theodoret gives information about his successive exiles, first to Arados, then to Oxyrhynchus, and finally to Philae in the far south of Egypt (*Ecclesiastical History* IV.16). He was also the recipient of two letters from Basil (Basil of Caesarea, *Letters* 264 and 267). For the probable significance of his appearance for the dating of Ma'in's activities, see the Introduction.

31 New Life: the phrase, common in Syriac authors, is derived from Peshitta Romans 6:4 (where the Greek has "newness of life").

Paul, the builder of the Church: not elsewhere in the Persian Martyr Acts, but compare Sahdona, *Book of Perfection* (ed. A. de Halleux, CSCO 254, 1965), IV, p. 53.

fight (*agona,* lit. "contest"): the term is used in quite a number of the Persian Martyr Acts, notably in Shem'on B (often) and Aqebshma (*AMS* II, 354–5, 377, 393–4).

32 Romania: for this term, see the Introduction. It does not occur in any of the other Persian Martyr Acts, but is occasionally found elsewhere, e.g. *AMS* VI, 537 (Domet), the Julian Romance (ed. G. Hoffmann; Leiden, 1880) 123, *Chronicle ad annum 819* (ed. A. Barsaum, CSCO 36, 1920), 13. An early East Syriac example is to be found in the historical introduction to the Acts of the Synod of Seleucia-Ctesiphon of 410, in *Synodicon Orientale*, ed. J-B. Chabot, (Paris, 1902), 18, line 23: "in the territory of R(h)omania."

the victorious king: likewise **47**, **60**, **62**, **65**, **87**. Since this passage identifies "the believing man" with "the victorious king," whereas elsewhere "the believing man" is the nameless ambassador, perhaps one should emend the text slightly by prefixing *dalath,* i.e. "*of* the victorious king."

34 Christian (*naṣraya*): this is the term regularly used by the Sasanian authorities for Christians (in due course it was taken over into Arabic, *naṣara*). The term already occurs in the inscription of Kardir from shortly after 276, where it features in Middle Persian alongside a form derived from the Greek *Christianos* (Syriac *krestyana*). In this inscription, and perhaps sometimes also in the Syriac Martyr Acts, *naṣraya* seems to be used of indigenous Christians in the Persian Empire, whereas *krestyana* refers to Christians deported (in considerable numbers) from the Roman Empire and settled in the Persian Empire. Elsewhere this distinction is not kept, and in the present text (as often elsewhere) *naṣraya* is only used when non-Christians are presented as speaking, whereas Christians are represented as using *krestyana* (note the transition between **39** and **40**).[18]

[18] For a recent discussion, see C. and F. Jullien, "Aux frontières de l'iranité: 'nasraye' et 'kristyone' des inscriptions du mobad Kirdir: enquête littéraire et historique," *Numen* 49 (2002): 282–335; also S. P. Brock, "Some Aspects of Greek Words in Syriac," in *Synkretismus im syrisch-persischen Kulturgebiet*, ed. A. Dietrich

38 tyrant: also used of the marzban in **52**; the term (especially common in Eusebius's *Martyrs of Palestine*) features occasionally in other Shapur Martyr Acts, e.g. Shem'on B 9, 37; *AMS* II, 250 (of Satan).

39 the governors (*mdabbrane*) of the world: this description of the sun and the moon is not found in any of the other Persian Martyr Acts, and would appear to have in mind astrological ideas, and not any form of Mazdaism; thus "celestial governors" feature in the *Book of the Laws of the Countries* 19 (ed. F. Nau, Patrologia Syriaca II, col. 568), and in 46 (Patr. Syr. II, col. 608) the term *mdabbrane* is in connection with fate.

Zeus ... Nanai ... Nabu ... Bel: Zeus is of course completely inappropriate, and elsewhere in the Persian Martyr Acts only occurs in the *History of Saba* (*AMS* II, 656). Nanai is equated with Artemis in a Greek votive inscription found in the Piraeus (Athens),[19] referred to by Hoffmann who devotes an extended note to her (pp. 130–39). At Palmyra Nanai is portrayed as Artemis on a tessera,[20] and the same identification is implicit in Josephus's reference to a temple of Artemis in Elymais (Susiana; *Antiquities* XII.354), corresponding to 2 Maccabees 1:13, which has "the temple of Nanaia." In ancient Mesopotamia she was especially associated with Nabu, and this is reflected in Strabo (*Geography* XVI.1.7) when he states that Borsippa was sacred to Artemis and Apollo (i.e. Nanai and Nabu). Elsewhere in the Persian Martyr Acts Nanai only appears in the *History of Karka d-Beth Slok* (*AMS* II, 516). As Fiey (p. 449) points out, Zeus, Nanai, Nabu and Bel are all inappropriate deities for Shapur to cite, and are better suited to a location in NW Mesopotamia. Nabu and Bel do not feature anywhere else in the Persian Martyr Acts.[21]

(Abhandlungen der Akademie der Wissenschaften in Göttingen, phil.-hist. Kl., III.96; 1975), esp. 91–95 (repr. in *Syriac Perspectives on Late Antiquity* [London, 1984], chapter IV). In the *Life of Simeon the Stylite*, according to the Vatican manuscript, ed. S. E. Assemani, *ASM* II, 329, we find the explicit statement that a Magus asked the Persian king for permission to imprison and forcibly convert "*krestyane*, whom they (sc. the Persians) call *nasraye*" (section 68 in R. Doran's translation, *The Lives of Simeon Stylites* [Kalamazoo, 1992], 148).

[19] *Inscriptiones Graecae* III.1, *Inscriptiones Atticae Aetatis Romanae* (Berlin, 1878), no. 131.

[20] H. Ingholt, H. Seyrig, J. Starcky, *Receuil des tessères de Palmyre* (Paris, 1955), no. 285. She is also mentioned on no. 238. For her, see J. Teixidor, *The Pantheon of Palmyra* (Leiden, 1979), 111–13.

[21] They feature together on another tessera from Palmyra, no. 137; see also Teixidor, *Pantheon*, 1–18 (Bel), 106–11 (Nabu).

sorcerer: a quite frequent accusation in the Persian Martyr Acts.

40 Christians (*krestyane*): the first occurrence of this term of Greek origin; hitherto *naṣraye* has always been used for "Christians," this being the standard term in use by the Persian authorities (see above, on **34**). The sudden appearance of *krestyana* here is not surprising, since it is in the mouth of Ma'in; later on, where *krestyana* is regularly used, the context is that of the Roman ambassador.

endurance (*msaybranuta*) (also **82**): a standard virtue in Martyr literature, but in the Shapur Martyr Acts it is only found in Shem'on A 43, B 88, and Aqebshma (*AMS* II, 356, 360, 372, 394). In the Peshitta New Testament it normally represents Greek *hupomonē*.

42 that deceiver (*maṭ'yana*): this perhaps deliberately reflects the use of the same term with reference to Christ in Matt 27:63.

45 salt and vinegar: similarly in the Acts of Dado (*AMS* IV, 219).

asafoetida (*ḥlṭyt'*; also **64**): so Hoffmann, who (note 237) states that this is thapsia asclepium (an umbellifer), and this is followed by K. Brockelmann in his *Lexicon* (Halle, 1928), though the basis for this identification is unclear. The word also occurs in E. A. Wallis Budge, *The Syriac Book of Medicines*, p. 318, where it is mentioned in connection with coldness of stomach. Evidently it is the same as *ḥltyt'* (with *tau*, not *ṭeth*),[22] also identified as "asafoetida" (I. Löw, *Aramäische Pflanzennamen* [Leipzig, 1881; repr. Hildesheim, 1973], 36), which is a gum with an unpleasant smell, produced from the root of ferula asafoetida).

Walgash: not otherwise known.

46 to receive tribute from him: this is clearly wishful thinking, seeing that it was normally the Romans who paid subsidies to the Persians (sometimes claimed by the Persians to be tribute),[23] in order for them to guard the Caucasian Gates against incursions of the Huns.[24] A similar example of

---

[22] This is implicit from the entries for the two words in R. Payne Smith's *Thesaurus Syriacus* (Oxford, 1879), where they are both identified as Silphium (Greek *silphion*, another species of ferula, though sometimes used with reference to asafoetida).

[23] A conception that the author of the *Chronicle of Joshua the Stylite* (section 9) was insistent on refuting: "this was not because [Peroz] could levy tribute" from the Romans.

[24] See R. C. Blockley, "Subsidies and diplomacy: Rome and Persia in Late Antiquity," *Phoenix* (Toronto) 39 (1985): 62–74.

wishful thinking, likewise claiming that Constantine received tribute from Shapur II, is to be found in the world chronicle of John of Nikiu, dating from the late seventh century.[25]

48 missives: perhaps the author has in mind the letter of Constantine to Shapur (of a very different character), recorded by Eusebius in his *Life of Constantine* (IV.8–13).[26]

hostage (*hmayra*): the term is found elsewhere in the Persian Martyr Acts in Aqebshma (*AMS* II, 374), where the daughter of the king of Armenia is held *ba-hmayre* in Maday (Media). According to Lee (who refers specifically to this passage, based on Hoffmann's summary) the situation described here is not typical of what seems to have been the normal situation with hostages.[27] For a surprising use of the term "hostage" in christology, see S. P. Brock, "Christ 'the Hostage': a theme in the East Syriac liturgical tradition and its origin," in *Logos. Festschrift für Luise Abramowski*, ed. H. C. Brennecke, E. L. Grasmück and C. Markschies (Beiheft ZNTW 67; Berlin, 1993), 472–85; repr. in *Fire from Heaven: Studies in Syriac Theology and Liturgy* (Aldershot, 2006), ch. IV.

53 appeared to him: similarly in the Acts of Mar Qardag (28) the ascetic 'Abdisho' appears to Qardag in a night vision.

was ... whisked away (*etgzez*): literally "he was cut off".

54 Greeks (*ywny'*): Hoffmann, note 243 suggests that this should be emended to "Chionites" (*kywny'*), who are specifically glossed as "that is, Huns" in the *Chronicle of Joshua the Stylite* (section 9),[28] against whom Peroz conducted campaigns in the late 5th century. The Chionites are mentioned by Ammianus Marcellinus (XVI.9–3–4) as making incursions into Shapur's territory in the time of Constantius, c. 356, though subsequently a peace treaty was arranged (XVII.5.1), while Gumbates, the

---

[25] Section 80.3 in R. H. Charles, *The Chronicle of John, Bishop of Nikiu* (London, 1916); a little later, in 80.35, the author makes the even more unrealistic claim that Jovian also received tribute from Shapur!

[26] For this, see T. D. Barnes, "Constantine and the Christians of Persia," *Journal of Roman Studies* 75 (1985): 126–36.

[27] See A. D. Lee, "The role of hostages in Roman diplomacy with Sasanian Persia," *Historia* 40 (1991): 366–74, esp. 372.

[28] Nöldeke suggested emending to "Kushans," and was followed in this by Wright; see, however, note 37 (p. 9) in F. R. Trombley and J. W. Watt, *The Chronicle of Pseudo-Joshua the Stylite* (Liverpool, 2000).

king of the Chionites, later assisted Shapur in his invasion of Mesopotamia and in the siege of Amida in 359 (XVIII.6.22; XIX.1.7 and XIX.2.3). There seems to be no clear evidence of the Huns causing trouble to the Persians again until the serious incursions of 395,[29] though around the mid 370s they had attacked the Alans in the region between the Sea of Azov and the Caucasus (Ammianus Marcellinus XXXI.3.1). On the whole it is probably best to keep to the reading of the manuscript and suppose that the passage alludes to the warfare in Armenia in the early 370s; for this, see above, in the Introduction, under Historicity.

55 sacrifice to the gods: the language would have been applicable to persecutions in the Roman Empire, but is not appropriate for the situation in Persia; this is another indication that the author is writing in the Roman Empire.

57 (torture) combs (*sraqe*): this form of torture (already foretold in **27** by Benjamin) would appear to be more typical of the Roman Empire, where it frequently turns up in martyr acts. In the Persian Martyr Acts it only features in the *Martyrdom of Gubralaha and Qazo* (*AMS* IV, 149), those of the two Sabas (*AMS* II, 639 and IV, 242), and the *History of Karka d-Beth Slok* (*AMS* II, 519, 525, 530).

through God's working (*ma'bdanuta*): the slightly different phrase "divine working" features in the *Martyrdom of Pusai* (*AMS* II, 230) and that of Sulṭan Mahduk (*AMS* II, 5, 6).

57–58 A similar case where a Roman ambassador secures the release of a Christian prisoner is to be found in Theodoret, *Ecclesiastical History*, V.39 (the man released is named Benjamin; this will presumably have featured in the lost part of the Syriac acts of ʻAbda).

60 palace: here and in **76** the less frequent spelling *pwlṭyn* is found (rather than the normal *plṭyn*). The term is used in a Persian context in some other Shapur Martyr Acts, e.g. *AMS* II 210 (Pusai; of Shapur II), and 238 (Martha; of the Chief Mobed).

---

[29] This is the subject of one of Cyrillona's poems. French translation in D. Cerbelaud, *L'Agneau véritable* (Chevetogne, 1984), IV.72–87); the Syriac text was published by G. Bickell in the *Zeitschrift der deutschen morgenländischen Geselschaft* 27 (1873): 583–93.

64 For the refusal of a doctor and of medicaments, compare Aqebshma (*AMS* II, 377).

65 tribunal (*bim*) of Christ: the absolute form is used, as Rom 14:10 and 2 Cor 5:10; contrast **77** (see note there).

67 investigation (*ziṭima* < Greek *zētēma*): the loanword is not otherwise found in the Shapur Martyr Acts, but already occurs several times in Peshitta Acts (18:15, 23:29, 25:19, 26:2).

68 he made him a bishop: the narrative requires this action since Ma'in is subsequently described as providing his monastic foundations with priests. According to canon law, of course, bishop Barse should have been accompanied by two other bishops (Council of Nicaea, Canon 4).

you shall see me in spirit twice: this is again alluded to in **76**.

71 'Anat: modern 'Ana, for which see note 8, above. A. Musil, *The Middle Euphrates* (New York, 1927), 18, note 14 (cf. p. 345) suggests that the site of Ma'in's cell where he spent seven years was al-Mašhad al-Jabir, which he states was a former Christian monastery, an hour and a half on foot from 'Ana.

72 lion: lions turn up not infrequently as companions of saints in Syriac hagiography (and of course elsewhere). A well-known example is provided by the association of Jerome with a lion in medieval Western European art, though this arose from a late development in the hagiographical tradition. Another popular saint associated with a lion is Mamas, who is depicted on icons as riding on a lion (thus also in his Life, *AMS* VI, 441). Eulogius, a disciple of Mar Awgen, likewise went around riding on a lion according to his life (unpublished; see Harvard Syr. 38, ff.108–9).

(once) with it: this seems to be the sense of *w-'ameh*, though possibly, in view of the next *'ameh*, *w-'ameh* should be deleted as an erroneous anticipation.

73 Agrippos (*'grpws*): as Fiey (447, n. 43) pointed out, *'grpws* is a corruption of *'wrpws*, Europos, then, on the basis of the corrupted form, a link with king Agrippa was subsequently provided. The related spelling *'grwpws* for Europos is also found in British Library, Add. 14, 533, in the list of signatories to Severus's *Prosphonesis* (ed. M. Kugener, PO 2.3 [1907]: 238–

41, and with commentary, in *Oriens Christianus* 2 [1902]: 265–82).[30] The *g* is also present in its modern name, Gerablus. Ma'in is thus represented, not only as moving a long way north, up the Euphrates, but also as finally settling within the Roman Empire(as he himself foretells in **63**). Europos is on the west bank of the Euphrates (close to the modern frontier between Turkey and Syria), and the famous monastery of Qenneshre cannot have been far away, on the east bank.

Shadwa: evidently the same as Shadbo in **91**. Fiey suggests that this is Shadabe, mentioned by R. Dussaud, *Topographie historique de la Syrie antique et mediévale* (Paris, 1927), 468.

two parasangs or six miles: it is interesting to note that R. Payne Smith already cited this passage (from Hoffmann) in the *Thesaurus Syriacus.*

decree of Constantine: here the author clearly envisages that all this takes place in Roman territory, and he retrojects Theodosius I's antipagan legislation to the time of Constantine.

revelry, of singing and drums: a similar combination of terms is found in the *Martyrdom of Sharbel* (W. Cureton, ed., *Ancient Syriac Documents*, [London, 1864], 40); the reverse order features in the *Martyrdom of Hyperechius* (in Samosata; *AMS* IV, 89 = *ASM* II, 121).

77 troubled by demons: the description in **77** and **81–82** of what would in modern terms be described as lasting trauma in the form of nightmares suffered by torture survivors is unique in the Persian Martyr Acts.

tribunal (*b'ima*): the use of this term, applicable only in the Roman Empire, is one of the various indications that the Acts of Ma'in were composed in the Roman Empire. The only other Shapur Martyr Acts where the term *bema* is used in a Persian context are the *History of Mar Saba* (*AMS* II, 658–9).

79 all the more cruel: the first *yattir* is awkwardly placed, and perhaps it should be deleted as another erroneous anticipation.

86 he addressed God in a loud voice: final prayers are quite frequently put into the mouths of martyrs and confessors.

89 our brethren: an indication that the *History* was written in a monastery said to have been founded by Mar Ma'in. As Fiey points out (p. 450)

[30] See Wright, *Catalogue*, 970.

Shadbo/Shadwa was probably not far from the famous monastery of Qenneshre.

INDEX OF NAMES

References are to section numbers of the text.

Index of Biblical References

References are to section numbers of the text. Direct quotations are indicated by italics.

APPENDIX

A GUIDE TO THE PERSIAN MARTYR ACTS

ABBREVIATIONS:

AB	*Analecta Bollandiana*
AG	Anno Graecorum (Seleucid era)
AMS	P. Bedjan, *Acta Martyrum et Sanctorum,* I-VII (Paris/Leipzig, 1890–1897).
AS	*Acta Sanctorum*
ASM	S. E. Assemani, *Acta Sanctorum et Martyrum*, I-II (Rome, 1748).
Bedjan, *Histoire de Mar Jabalaha...*	P. Bedjan, *Histoire de Mar Jabalaha, de trois autres patriarches, d'un prêtre et de deux laïques, nestoriens* (Leipzig/Paris, 1895; repr. as *The History of Mar-Jabalaha and Rabban Sauma*, Gorgias Historical Texts 14; Piscataway, NJ, 2007).
BHO	*Bibliotheca Hagiographica Orientalis* (Bruxelles, 1914).
Braun	O. Braun, *Ausgewählte Akten persischer Märtyrer* (Kempten/München, 1915).
Brock-Harvey, *Holy Women*	S. P. Brock and S. A. Harvey, *Holy Women of the Syrian Orient* (Berkeley, 1987).
Crucifixion	Year since the crucifixion
ET	English translation
FT	French translation
GT	German translation
HE	*Historia Ecclesiastica*
Hoffmann	G. Hoffmann, *Auszüge aus syrischen Akten persischer Märtyrer* (Abhandlungen für die Kunde des Morgenlandes 7:3; Leipzig, 1880)
LT	Latin translation
PO	Patrologia Orientalis
PO II	Patrologia Orientalis II.4, H. Delehaye, *Les versions grecques des martyrs persans sous Sapor II* (Paris, 1905).
PS I.2	*Patrologia Syriaca* I.2, M. Kmosko, ed., *S. Simeon bar Sabba'e*, cols 660–1055.
Sas	Sasanian Regnal Year

Sims-Williams N. Sims-Williams, *The Christian Sogdian Manuscript C2* (Schriften zur Geschichte und Kultur des Alten Orients; Berlin, 1985).

SynCp H. Delehaye, *Synaxarium Ecclesiae Constantinopolitanae* (Bruxelles, 1902).

(1) SYRIAC TEXTS

Note: French translations, made from Latin, of texts in *ASM* I can be found in F. Lagrange, *Les Actes des Martyrs d'Orient* (Paris, 1852). Arabic translations of many of the texts are provided in [A. Scher], *Kitab sirat ashhar shuhada' al-Mashriq al-qiddisin* (2 vols, Mosul 1900, 1906).

Under Vahran II (276–293)

1. CANDIDA: ed. with ET, S. P. Brock, *AB* 96 (1978): 167–81 (repr. in S. P. Brock, *Syriac Perspectives on Late Antiquity* [London, 1984], chapter IX).

Under Shapur II (309–379)

Shapur year 9:

2. SULṬAN MAHDUKT/MARTYRS of TUR BER'AIN, *BHO 1106* [Shapur year 9, 12 Kanun II]: *AMS* II, 1–39; German summary: Hoffmann, 9–16.

Shapur year 18:

3. ZEBINA and companions, *BHO* 531 [Shapur year 18, 29 lunar Kanun I]: *AMS* II, 39–51; *ASM* I, 215–24; Greek: PO II, nos. 1–2 (and earlier, in *AB* 22 (1903): 395–407); *SynCp* 29 Mar.

Shapur year 23:

4. GUBRALAHA and QAZO, *BHO* 325 [Shapur year 23, 22 lunar Illul]: *AMS* IV, 141–63. Greek: *Acta Sanctorum,* September VIII (Antwerp, 1762), 127–35.

Shapur year 30:

5. Pr SHABUR of Niqator and bp ISAAC of Karka d-Beth Slok, *BHO* 1042 [Shapur year 30]: *AMS* II, 51–56; *ASM* I, 226–29; *AS* Nov IV, 429–32 (Vat. Syr. 161). GT Braun, 1–4.

Shapur year 31:

6. SHEM'ON bar ṢABBA'E, A, *BHO* 1117 [Shapur 31 = Sas 117, 14 Nisan; Karka d-Ledan]: PS I.2, 715–78; *AMS* II, 123–30 (opening only, §1–9 in *PS*); *ASM* I, 10–36. Armenian: *BHO* 1118.
7. SHEM'ON bar ṢABBA'E, B, *BHO* 1119 [Shapur 31 = Sas 117 = AG 655 = Crucifixion 296]: PS I.2, 779–960; *AMS* II, 131–207. Greek: So-

zomen, *HE* II.10 (see P. Devos, *AB* 84 (1966): 443–56). Greek: *SynCp* 17 Apr. GT Braun, 5–57.

8. POSI (PUSAI), *BHO* 993 [Shapur 31, Saturday, 15 Nisan; Karka d-Ledan]: *AMS* II, 208–32. Greek: Sozomen, *HE* II.11 (17 Apr.); GT Braun, 58–75.

9. MARTHA, *BHO* 698 [Shapur 31, Sunday 16 Nisan; with a reference to Vahram year 8 = 89 years later; Karka d-Ledan]: *AMS* II, 233–41. Greek: cf. Sozomen, *HE* II.11. ET Brock-Harvey, *Holy Women*, 67–73; GT Braun, 76–82.

10. GREAT SLAUGHTER, *BHO* 704 [Shapur 31, Monday through Saturday in the week after Easter; Karka d-Ledan]: *AMS* II, 241–48; GT Braun, 83–88.

11. TARBO, *BHO* 1149 [Shapur 31, 5 lunar Iyyar]: *AMS* II, 254–60; *ASM* I, 54–59. Greek: Sozomen, *HE* II.12; PO II, no. 3; *SynCp* 5 Apr.; Sogdian: Sims-Williams; ET Brock-Harvey, *Holy Women*, 73–76; GT Braun, 89–92. On the Greek translation: N. Pigulevskaya, in *Festschrift für F. Altheim*, II (Berlin, 1970), 96–100.

Shapur year 32:

12. AZAD, *BHO* 124 [Shapur 32, Nisan]: *AMS* II, 248–54; *ASM* I, 45–50. Greek: Sozomen, *HE* II.11.

Persecution year 2:

13. SHAHDOST, *BHO* 1033 [Persecution 2, 20 lunar Shebaṭ; Beth Lapaṭ]: *AMS* II, 276–81; *ASM* I, 88–91; Greek PO II, no. 4 (and earlier in *AB* 21 (1902): 141–7; *SynCp* 19 Oct., 20 Feb. Sogdian: Sims-Williams. GT Braun, 93–96.

Persecution year 4:

14. Bp JOHN of ARBELA, *BHO* 500 [Persecution 4, 1 lunar Teshri II; Beth Lapaṭ]: *AMS* IV, 128–30. Greek: *SynCp* 1 Nov.

15. Bp NARSAI and JOSEPH, *BHO* 806 [Persecution 4, 10 lunar Teshri II; Ṣepta]: *AMS* II, 284–86; *ASM* I, 97–99; *AS* Nov. IV 425–29 (< Vat. Syr. 160). Greek: *SynCp* 20 Nov.

Persecution year 5:

16. Bp ABRAHAM of ARBELA, *BHO* 12 [Persecution 5, 5 lunar Shebaṭ; Tell Nyaḥa]: *AMS* IV, 130–31; Greek: PO II, nos. 5–6; *SynCp* 5 Feb. Coptic: *Proceedings of the Society for Biblical Archaeology* 30 (1908): 234–7, 276–8.

17. 111 MEN and 9 WOMEN, *BHO* 718 [Persecution 5, 6 lunar Nisan; Seleucia-Ctesiphon]: *AMS* II, 291–95; *ASM* I, 105–109. Greek: *SynCp* 5 Apr. Sogdian: Sims-Williams. GT Braun, 97–99.

Persecution year 6:

18. BARBA'SHMIN, *BHO* 135 [Persecution 6, 9 Kanun II; Karka d-Ledan]: *AMS* II, 296–303; *ASM* I, 111–16. Sogdian: Sims-Williams. GT Braun, 100–104.

19. ḤNANYA, *BHO* 372 [Persecution 6, 12 lunar Kanun]: *AMS* IV, 131–32. Greek: *SynCp* 1 Dec.

Persecution year 7:

20. Pr JACOB and MARY, *BHO* 426 [Persecution 7, 17 lunar Adar; Tell Dara, on the Greater Zab]: *AMS* II, 307; *ASM* I, 122. GT Braun, 105.

Seleucid era 662:

21. MARTYRS of GILAN, *BHO* 180, 1043 [AG 662, Thursday, 12 Nisan; on the Euphrates]: *AMS* IV, 166–70 (end lost).

Seleucid era 663:

22. BEHNAM and SARAH, *BHO* 177 [10 Kanun I; AG 663, "time of Julian"!]: *AMS* II, 397–441. On this text, see G. Wiessner, *Synkretismusforschung* (Wiesbaden, 1978), 119–33, and H. Younansardaroud, in *Syriaca*, ed. M. Tamcke (Münster, 2002), 185–96.

Persecution year 15:

23. Dcn BARḤADBESHABBA of Arbela, *BHO* 138 [Persecution 15, 20 lunar Tammuz; Ḥazza]: *AMS* II, 314–16.

24. Pr AITALLAHA and dcn ḤOPHSAI, *BHO* 29 [Persecution 15, 16 lunar Kanun; Beth Huzzaye]: *AMS* IV, 133–37. Greek: *SynCp* 11 Dec.

25. THEKLA and companions, *BHO* 1157 [Persecution 15, 6 lunar Ḥaziran; Ḥazza]: *AMS* II, 308–13; *ASM* I, 123–27. Greek: *SynCp* 9 Jun. ET Brock-Harvey, *Holy Women*, 78–81. GT Braun, 106–109.

Shapur year 49:

26. QARDAG, *BHO* 555–6 [Shapur 49]: *AMS* II, 442–506; Abbeloos (+ LT) *AB* 9 (1890), 5–106. ET in J. Walker, *The Legend of Mar Qardag* (Berkeley, 2006), 19–69.

Shapur year 53:

27. CAPTIVES from BETH ZABDAI, *BHO* 375 [Shapur 53]: *AMS* II, 316–24; *ASM* I,134–40. Greek: Sozomen, *HE* II.13; PO II, nos. 7 (opening only); *SynCp* 9 Apr. GT Braun, 110–15.

28. SABA, *BHO* 1031 [Shapur 53 = AG 674 = Crucifixion 324]: *AMS* IV, 222–49.

Persecution year 32:

29. Pr JACOB and dcn AZAD, *BHO* 423 [Persecution 32, 14 Nisan; Arbela]: *AMS* IV, 137–41. Greek: *SynCp* 17 Apr.

Persecution year 36:

30. FORTY MARTYRS, *BHO* 5 [Persecution 36, 15/22 lunar Iyyar; Karka d-Ledan, Beth Lapaṭ]: *AMS* II, 325–47; *ASM* I, 144–63. Greek: *SynCp* 16 May.

Persecution year 37:

31. ʿAQEBSHMA, *BHO* 22 [Persecution 37, Thursday, The Second Week of Pentecost; Beth Ṭabbaḥe (Arbela)]: *AMS* II, 351–96; *ASM* I,171–208. Greek: Sozomen, *HE* II.13; PO II, nos. 10–13; *SynCp* 3 Nov. Armenian: *BHO* 23. GT Braun, 116–38.

No year given [in alphabetical order]:

32. BADAY, *BHO* 130 [5 lunar Teshri I]: *AMS* IV, 163–65.

33. BADMA abbot, *BHO* 131 [10 lunar Nisan]: *AMS* II, 347–51; *ASM* I 165–68. Greek: PO II, no. 9; *SynCp* 9 Apr.

34. BARSHEBYA, *BHO* 146 [17 lunar Ḥaziran]: *AMS* II, 281–4; *ASM* I, 93–95.

35. DADU, *BHO* 240: *AMS* IV, 218–21 (beginning lost); German summary: Hoffmann 33–34.

36. DANIEL and WARDA, *BHO* 245 [25 lunar Shebaṭ; 2 years after Miles]: *AMS* II, 290; *ASM* I, 103–104.

37. MAʿIN, *BHO* 753: present volume. German summary: Hoffmann 28–33; study by Fiey, *Le Muséon* 84 (1971): 437–53.

38. MARTYRS outside Court, *BHO* 711 [time of Barbaʿshmin's martyrdom = Persecution year 6]: *AMS* II, 303–306; *ASM* I, 118–20.

39. MARTYRS of BETH SLOK, *BHO* 807: *AMS* II, 286–89; *ASM* I, 99–101. Partial ET Brock-Harvey, *Holy Women*, 77.

40. MILES, *BHO* 772 [13 lunar Teshri II]: *AMS* II, 260–75; *ASM* I, 66–79. Greek: Sozomen, *HE* II.14; *SynCp* 13 Nov. Armenian: *BHO* 773.

(Only in Greek):

IA: PO II, nos. 7–8.

(Only in Armenian):

BARDISHO: *BHO* 136. ET L. H. Gray, *AB* 67 (1949): 361–76.

SERGIUS and MARTYRIUS: *BHO* 1056–8.

For the (damaged) list of Persian martyrs at the end of British Library, Add. 12, 150, copied in Edessa in November 411, see F. Nau, PO 10.1 (1912): 7–26, and the alphabetical list given after the indexes below (this includes a few further names which are preserved in Deir al-Surian Syriac Fragment no. 27).

Late fourth century

Undated

41. PINḤAS, *BHO* 989 [28 Nisan]: *AMS* IV, 208–18.

Seleucid era 699:

42. BASSUS and SUSANNA, *BHO* 174 [11 Iyyar, AG 699]: *AMS* IV, 471–507; J-B. Chabot, *La légende de Mar Bassus martyr persan* (Paris, 1893) (+ FT).

Seleucid era 701:

43. 'ABDALMASIḤ of Sinjar, *BHO* 3 [Friday 27 Tammuz, AG 701]: *AMS* I, 173–201; Corluy, AB 5 (1887): 5–52 (+ LT); cf. J-M. Fiey *Le Muséon,* 77 (1964): 205–23. Arabic (+ LT): P. Peeters, *AB* 44 (1926): 270–341. Armenian: *BHO* 4.

Under Yazdgard I (399–420)

44. 'ABDA, *BHO* 6: *AMS* IV, 250–53 (end lost). Greek: Theodoret, *HE* V.39; *SynCp* 17 Oct. Armenian: *BHO* 7; LT P. Peeters, *AB* 28 (1909): 399–415. GT Braun, 139–41; German summary: Hoffmann, 34–45.

45. 10 MARTYRS of Beth GARMAI, *BHO* 387 [Seleucia-Ctesiphon]: *AMS* IV, 184–88.

46. NARSAI, *BHO* 786 [Seleucia-Ctesiphon]: *AMS* IV, 170–80. GT Braun 142–49; German summary: Hoffmann, 36–8. FT P. Devos, *AB* 93 (1965): 305–10.

47. ṬAṬAQ, *BHO* 1139 [Seleucia-Ctesiphon]: *AMS* IV, 181–84.

Under Vahram V (421–438)

48. JACOB INTERCISUS, *BHO* 294 [Friday, 27 Teshri II "of the Greeks," Vahram year 1/2, AG 732]: *AMS* II, 539–58; *ASM* I, 242–57. Greek: P. Devos, *AB* 71 (1953): 178–210, and 72 (1954): 213–56. Latin: *BHL* 4100. Armenian: *BHO* 395. Coptic: *BHO* 396–7. GT Braun, 150–62. LT of Syriac: P. Devos, *AB* 71 (1953): 168–78.

49. JACOB THE NOTARY, *BHO* 412 [Seleucia-Ctesiphon]: *AMS* IV, 189–200. GT Braun, 170–78.

50. MIHRSHABUR, *BHO* 771 [Vahram year 2, Saturday, Teshri I]: *AMS* II, 535–39; *ASM* I, 234–36.

51. PEROZ of Beth Lapaṭ, *BHO* 921 [Sirzur, 5 Illul "of the Greeks," Vahram 1, AG 733]: *AMS* IV, 253–62. GT Braun, 163–69; German summary: Hoffmann, 39–43.

Under Yazdgard II (439–457)[31]

52. ADHURHORMIZD and ANAHID, *BHO* 25, 47 [25 Nisan and 18 June, Yazdgard 9, Sas 223, AG 759]: *AMS* II, 583–603. Sogdian: Sims-Williams. ET (Anahid): Brock-Harvey, *Holy Women*, 82–99 (with further literature, p. 190).

53. MARTYRS of KARKA D-BETH SLOK, *BHO* 705: *AMS* II, 507–35. GT Braun 179–87, German summary: Hoffmann, 61–68. Partial ET, Brock-Harvey, *Holy Women*, 77–8. Cf. J. M. Fiey, *AB* 82 (1964): 189–222.

54. PETHION, *BHO* 923–4 [Yazdgard 9, AG 759]: *AMS* II, 604–31; J. Corluy *AB* 7 (1888): 5–44 (+ LT). Sogdian: Sims-Williams. Armenian: *BHO* 925.

55. YAZDIN, *BHO* 434: *AMS* II 559–83. Sogdian: Sims-Williams. German summary: Hoffmann, 61–68.

56. ṬAHMAZGARD, *BHO* 1138: H. Hilgenfeld, *Ausgewählte Gesänge des Giwargis Wards von Arbel* (Leipzig, 1904), 37–40.

Late fifth century

57. BABOI, *BHO* 126 [AD 484]: *AMS* II, 631–4.

58. SABA, *BHO* 1031 [d. Sas 261; AG 799]: *AMS* II, 635–80. German summary: Hoffmann, 68–78.[32]

Under Khosro I (531–579)

59. ABA, Mar, *BHO* 595: Bedjan, *Mar Jabalaha...*, 206–74, 274–87. GT Braun 188–220.

60. GREGORY (PIRANGUSHNASP), *BHO* 353: Bedjan, *Mar Jabalaha...*, 347–94. Armenian: *BHO* 354. German summary: Hoffmann, 78–86.

61. YAZDPANEH, *BHO* 431: Bedjan, *Mar Jabalaha...*, 394–415. German summary: Hoffmann, 87–91.

(Only in Greek):

SHIRIN (d. AD 559): P. Devos, *AB* 64 (1946): 87–131; FT *AB* 112 (1994): 4–31.

(Only in Armenian/Georgian):

---

[31] **52, 54,** and **55,** which all belong together, are listed here in alphabetic order; in *AMS* II Yazdin (**55**) features before **52** and **54**.

[32] Although this Saba is neither a martyr nor a confessor, he is included here since his life has clearly made use of the Martyrdom of Saba [= **28**]; note especially their final prayers.

MAKHOZ-YAZDBOZID (IZBOZETA): Armenian (*BHO* 433) and Georgian: *AS* Nov. IV, 204–13. (The Syriac fragment in British Library, Add. 17, 216, mentioning a Yazdbozid, published by P. Peeters, *AB* 49 (1931): 5–21, is not related to this, according to Fiey, *Saints syriaques*, 196, contrary to Peeters's suggestion).

Under Khosro I/Hormizd IV/Khosro II

(Only in Georgian):

GOLINDUSH (d. AD 591): Georgian: LT by G. Garitte, *AB* 74 (1956): 405–40. On this life, see P. Peeters, *AB* 63 (1944): 74–125.

Under Khosro II (591–628)

62. CHRISTINA (YAZDOY), *BHO* 187: *AMS* IV, 201–207 (fragment).

63. GEORGE (MIHRAMGUSHNASP), *BHO* 323: Bedjan, *Mar Jabalaha...*, 416–571; cf. J.-B. Chabot, *Synodicon Orientale* (Paris, 1902), 625–34. GT Braun, 221–77; German summary: Hoffmann, 91–2. On this life see G. J. Reinink in *Portraits of Spiritual Authority*, ed. J. Watt and J. W. Drijvers (Leiden, 1999), 171–93.

64. ISHO'SABRAN (MAHANOSH), *BHO* 451: J.-B. Chabot, *Nouvelles archives des mission scientifiques* 7 (1897): 503–84 + French summary. On this life see F. Jullien, *Res Orientales* 16 (2004): 171–81.

(Only in Greek and Latin):

ANASTASIUS (MOGUNDAT): B. Flusin, ed., *Saint Anastase le Perse et l'histoire de la Palestine au début du VIIe siècle* (2 vols, Paris, 1992).

Concordance with Bedjan, *AMS* II and IV

Bedjan, *AMS* II

1–39	Sulṭan Mahdukht	= **2**
39–51	Zebina	= **3**
51–56	Bp Shabur	= **5**
128–30	Shem'on bar Ṣabba'e, A	= **6** (beginning only)
131–207	Shem'on bar Ṣabba'e, B	= **7**
208–32	Posi	= **8**
233–41	Martha	= **9**
241–48	Great Slaughter	= **10**
248–54	Azad	= **12**
254–60	Tarbo	= **11**
260–75	Miles	= **40**
276–81	Shahdost	= **13**
281–84	Bar Shebya	= **34**
284–86	Bp Narse	= **15**
286–89	Martyrs of Beth Slok	= **39**
290	Daniel and Warda	= **36**
291–95	111 Men and 9 Women	= **17**
296–303	Barba'shmin	= **18**
303–6	Martyrs outside court	= **38**
307	Jacob and Mary	= **20**
308–13	Thekla	= **25**
314–16	Barḥadbeshabba	= **23**
316–24	Captives	= **27**
325–47	40 Martyrs	= **30**
347–51	Badma	= **33**
351–96	Bp 'Aqebshma	= **31**
397–441	Behnam and Sara	= **22**
442–506	Qardag	= **25**
507–35	Martyrs of Beth Slok	= **53**
535–39	Mihrshashabur	= **50**
539–58	Jacob Intercisus	= **48**
559–603	Adhurhormizd and Anahid	= **52**
604–31	Pethion	= **54**
631–34	Baboi	= **57**
635–80	Saba	= **58**

Bedjan, *AMS* IV

128–30	Bp John	= **14**
130–31	Bp Abraham	= **16**
131–32	Ḥnanya	= **19**
133–37	Aitallaha	= **24**
137–41	Jacob and Azad	= **29**
141–63	Gubralaha and Qazo	= **4**
163–65	Baday	= **32**
166–70	Martyrs of Gilan	= **21**
170–80	Narsai	= **46**
181–84	Ṭaṭaq	= **47**
184–88	10 Martyrs of Beth Garmai	= **45**
189–200	Jacob the Notary	= **49**
201–7	Christina	= **62**
208–18	Pinḥas	= **41**
218–21	Dadu	= **35**
222–49	Saba	= **28**
250–53	'Abda	= **44**
253–62	Peroz	= **51**
471–99	Bassus and Susanna	= **42**

(2) EARLY MANUSCRIPTS

Although Vatican Syr. 160 and 161, both old manuscripts, were used for *ASM,* for many of the additional texts in *AMS* II Bedjan used late manuscripts. The most important of these were two volumes copied in Mosul in 1869[33] from a manuscript once in the Chaldean Church in Diyarbakır[34] (the contents of these two volumes were listed by J. B. Abbeloos in *AB* 9 [1890]: 5–7, and by Assfalg; the only texts absent from this large collection are **1**, **2**, **12, 27, 30, 35, 37, 38, 42, 45, 52, 56, 57** and **60**). For *AMS* IV Bedjan made use of certain manuscripts in the British Library (formerly, British Museum), including Add. 7200. For the texts in *Histoire de Mar Jabalaha ...*, Bedjan used Abbeloos's two manuscripts of 1869. In several cases earlier manuscripts (albeit sometimes fragmentary) survive, mostly in the British Library, and for convenience all manuscripts prior to the thirteenth century that are available are also listed in the Table below. The dates of the manuscripts in question are:

Damascus,	Syr. Orth. Patr. 12/18	12th cent.
London,	Add. 7,200	12th/13th cent.
	Add. 12,142	6th cent,
	Add. 12,174	AD 1197
	Add. 14,644	5th/6th cent.
	Add. 14,645	AD 936
	Add. 14,654	6th cent.
	Add. 14,665	10th cent.
	Add. 14,733	AD 1199
	Add. 14,735	12th/13th cent.
	Add. 17,204	5th cent.

---

[33] These two manuscripts are now Berlin Or. Oct. 1256 and 1257, and are described by J. Assfalg, *Verzeichnis der orientalischen Handschriften in Deutschland,* V, *Syrische Handschriften* (Wiesbaden, 1963), 53–59. Bedjan's statement (*AMS* II, vii) that the manuscript was copied in 1879 is evidently an error, as the colophon clearly gives 1869.

[34] No. 96 in A. Scher's Catalogue, *Journal asiatique* X.10 (1907), 398–401; according to W. A. Macomber, this manuscript is now in the Chaldean Patriarchate, Baghdad: see his "New finds of Syriac manuscripts in the Middle East," in *XVII. Deutscher Orientalistentag,* ed. W. Voigt (Zeitschrift der Deutschen Morgenländischen Gesellschaft, Suppl. I,2; Wiesbaden, 1969), 480, no. 42. Although Bedjan (*AMS* II, vii) stated that the manuscript dated from the 7th or 8th century, Scher (p. 401) gave it as 11th or 12th century.

Add. 17,267	13th cent.
Paris, Syr. 234	13th cent.
Paris, Syr. 236	AD 1194
Vatican Syr. 160	6th cent.
Vatican Syr. 161	9th cent.

No.		Vat. Syr. 160	Vat. Syr. 161	Other early mss where available	Greek	Armenian	Sogdian
1	Candida			Add. 12,142			
2	Sultan Mahd.			Add. 12,174			
3	Zebina		*	Add. 14,654	PO II		
4	Gubralaha				*AS* Sep VIII		
5	Shabur		*	Add. 14,654			
6	Shem. b. Ṣab. A	*	*	Add. 14,645 Add. 14,665		*	
7	Shem. b. Sab. B		*	Add. 12,174	Soz. *SynCp*		
8	Posi			Add. 12,174	Soz.		
9	Martha			Add. 12,174	Soz.		
10	Gt Slaughter						
11	Tarbo	*	*	Add. 14,654 Add. 14,645 Add. 12,174	Soz. PO II		*
12	Azad				Soz.		
13	Shahdost		*	Add. 14,654 Add. 14,645 Add. 12,174	PO II		*
14	John				*SynCp*		
15	Narsai	*			*SynCp*		
16	Abraham				PO II		(Coptic)
17	111 men	*	*	Add. 14,654 Add. 12,174	*SynCp*		*
18	Barba'shmin	*	*	Add. 14,645			*
19	Ḥnanya				*SynCp*		
20	Jacob	*					
21	Mart. Gilan						

No.		Vat. Syr. 160	Vat. Syr. 161	Other early mss where available	Greek	Armenian	Sogdian
22	Behnam			Add. 7,200 Add. 12,174 Add. 14,733 Add. 14,735 Add. 17,267 Paris Syr. 234			
23	Barḥadbesh.	*		Add. 14,654			
24	Aitalaha	*			*SynCp*		
25	Thekla				*SynCp*		
26	Qardag						
27	Captives		*		Soz., PO II		
28	Saba			Add. 7,200			
29	Jacob						
30	XL Martyrs		*	Add. 14,645[35]	*SynCp*		
31	ʻAqebshma	*	*	Add. 14,654	Soz., PO II	*	
32	Baday						
33	Badma	*	*	Add. 14,654	PO II		
34	Barshebya	*	*	Add. 14,645			
35	Dadu			Add. 7,200			
36	Daniel	*	*				
37	Maʻin			Add. 12,174			
38	Martyrs		*				
39	Mart. B.Slok						
40	Miles	*	*	Add. 17,204 Add. 14,654 Add. 7,200	Soz. *SynCp*		
41	Pinḥas						
42	Bassus						
43	ʻAbda da-mshiḥa			Add. 12,174 Add. 17,267 Dam. 12/18		*	(Arabic)

[35] Add. 14,645 does not have the rhetorical prologue of *AMS* II, 325–32.

No.		Vat. Syr. 160	Vat. Syr. 161	Other early mss where available	Greek	Armenian	Sogdian
44	'Abda				Thdt	*	
45	X Mart.						
46	Narsai			Add. 7,200			
47	Ṭaṭaq						
48	Jacob Int.		*	Add. 14,644 Paris 234 Paris 236 Dam. 12/18	*	*	(Coptic)
49	Jacob Not.			Add. 7,200			
50	Mihrshabur		*				
51	Peroz			Add. 7,200			
52	Adhurhormizd						*
53	Mart. B. Slok			Add. 7,200			
54	Pethion			Add. 12,174 Dam. 12/18		*	*
55	Yazdin						
56	Ṭahmazgard						
57	Baboi						
58	Saba			Add. 7,200			
59	Aba						
60	Gregory			Add. 7,200		*	
61	Yazdpaneh			Add. 7,200			
62	Christina						
63	George			Add. 7,200			
64	Isho'sabran		*				

(3) GREEK TRANSLATIONS

Notices concerning Persian martyrs under Shapur II are to be found in the ecclesiastical histories by Theodoret (*HE*, V.39) and by Sozomen (*HE*, II.9), who could already be using Greek translations of selected martyrdoms. Descendants of these translations feature in certain manuscripts of menologia, and the texts for martyrs under Shapur II were edited from these sources by H. Delehaye in PO II.4.[36] Short summaries are also to be found in synaxaria, and references to these are given in **(1)** above by date, based on Delehaye's edition of the *Synaxarium Ecclesiae Constantinopolitanae.* The fuller texts in PO II are the following, with the corresponding texts in Syriac (in some cases there are different forms of the Greek):

nos. 1–2	Ionas and Barichisios	*AMS* II, 39–52 (= **3**)
no. 3	Pherbouthes[37]	*AMS* II, 254–60 (= **11**)
no. 4	Sadoth	*AMS* II, 276–81 (= **13**)
nos. 5–6	Bishop Abraham	*AMS* IV, 130–31 (= **16**)
nos. 7–8	Ia	(Only the opening of no. 7 corresponds to *AMS* II, 316–7 (= **27**))
no. 9	Bademos	*AMS* II, 347–51 (= **33**)
nos. 10–13	Akepsimas	*AMS* II, 351–96 (= **31**)

[36] Delehaye mentions (p. 6), but did not include, the *Martyrdom of Dada, Gobdela and Kasdia,* for which he did not know any Syriac equivalent; in fact it corresponds to *AMS* IV, 141–63 (= **4**).

[37] See also N. Pigulevskaya, "Syrischer Texte und griechische Übersetzung der Märtyren-Akten der heiligen Tarbo," in *Beiträge zur Alten Geschichte und deren Nachleben. Festschrift für F. Altheim,* ed. R. Stiehl and H. E. Stier (Berlin, 1970), II, 96–100.

(4) SELECT BIBLIOGRAPHY

Note: The following list is confined to works specifically dealing with the martyrdoms (works already mentioned above are not repeated here); for the general background of the Sasanian Empire, A. Christensen, *L'Iran sous les Sasanides* (2nd edn; Copenhagen, 1944) remains basic, even though it needs updating in several respects. More recent surveys can be found in E. Yarshater, ed., *The Cambridge History of Iran,* 3:1–2, *The Seleucid, Parthian and Sasanian Periods* (Cambridge, 1983), K. Schippmann, *Grundzüge der Geschichte des sasanidischen Reiches* (Darmstadt, 1990), and Part IV of J. Wieshofer, *Ancient Persia* (London, 1996; 2nd edn, 2001). For relations between the two empires, see B. Dignas and E. Winter, *Rome and Persia in Late Antiquity* (Cambridge, 2007), while excerpts from ancient sources are given in M. H. Dodgeon and S. N. C. Lieu, *The Roman Frontier and the Persian Wars, AD 226–363* (London, 1991), and G. Greatrex and S. N. C. Lieu, *The Roman Frontier and the Persian Wars, AD 363–630* (London, 2002), where further bibliography can be found.

Short (but usually good) entries on many of the martyrs can be found in *Bibliotheca Sanctorum*, 1–15 (Rome, 1961–2000), *Dictionnaire d'histoire et de géographie ecclésiastiques* (1912–), *Enciclopedia dei Santi: le Chiesi Orientali*, I-II (Rome, 1998–9), and the second edition of the *Lexikon für Theologie und Kirche* (1993–2001).

Among ancient sources, besides the passages in Theodoret and Sozomen, the *Chronicle of Seert* (ed. A. Scher, PO 4, 5, 7 and 13) and the problematic *Chronicle of Arbela* (ed. Kawerau, CSCO 467–8, 1985) are of course also of relevance.

Braun, O. – see under Abbreviations.

Brock, S. P., "Christians in the Sasanid Empire: a case of divided loyalties," in *Religion and National Identity*, ed. S. Mews (Studies in Church History 18; Oxford, 1982), 1–19 (reprinted in Brock, *Syriac Perspectives on Late Antiquity* [London, 1984], chapter 6).

Burgess, R. W., "The dates of the martyrdom of Simeon bar Sabba'e and the 'Great Massacre,'" *AB* 117 (1999): 9–47.

Chaumont, M-L., *La christianisation de l'empire iranien des origines aux grandes persécutions du IVe siècle* (CSCO 499, Subsidia 80; Louvain, 1988).

Decret, F., "Les conséquences sur le christianisme en Perse de l'affrontement des empires romain et sassanide. De Shapur Ie à Yazdgard Ie," *Recherches augustiniennes* 14 (1979): 91–152.

Devos, P., "Commémoraisons de martyrs persans dans le synaxaire de Lund," *AB* 81 (1963): 143–58.

———, "Abgar: hagiographe perse méconnu (début du Ve siècle)," *AB* 83 (1965): 303–28.

———, "Les martyrs persans à travers leurs actes syriaques," *Atti del convegno sul tema La Persia e il mondo Greco-Romano* (Rome, 1966), 213–25.

———, "Notes d'hagiographie perse," *AB* 84 (1966): 229–46.

Fiey, J-M., "Persécutions," in his *Jalons pour une histoire de l'Église en Iraq* (CSCO 310; Subsidia 36; Louvain, 1970), 85–99.

Fiey, J-M. (ed. L. I. Conrad), *Saints syriaques* (Studies in Late Antiquity and Early Islam 6; Princeton, 2004).

Follieri, E., "Santi persiani nell'innografia byzantina," *Atti del convegno sul tema La Persia e il mondo Greco-Romano* (Rome, 1966), 227–42.

Gignoux, Ph., "Titres et fonctions religieuses sasanides d'après les sources syriaques," *Acta Antiqua Academiae Scientiarum Hungaricae* 28 (1980): 191–203 (repr. in J. Harmatta, ed., *From Hecataeus to al-Huwarizmi* (Budapest, 1984), 191–203).

———, "Éléments de prosopographie de quelques Mobads sasanides," *Journal asiatique* 270 (1982): 257–69.

———, "Sur quelques relations entre chrétiens et mazdéens d'après les sources syriaques," *Studia Iranica* 28 (1999): 83–94.

———, "Une typologie des miracles des saints et martyrs perses dans l'Iran sassanide," in *Miracle et Karama. Hagiographies médiévales comparée, 2*, ed. D. Aigle (Turnhout, 2000), 499–523.

Gignoux, Ph., and Jullien, C., "L'onomastique iranienne dans les sources syriaques," *Parole de l'Orient* 31 (2006): 279–94.

Guidi, I, "Indice agiografico degli Acta Martyrum et Sanctorum," *Rendiconti della Reale Accademia dei Lincei* 28 (1919): 207–29.

Higgins, M. J., "The date of the martyrdom of Simeon bar Sabbae," *Traditio* 11 (1955): 1–35.

Hoffmann, G. – see under Abbreviations.

Jullien, C., "Contributions des Actes des martyrs perses à la géographie historique et à l'administration de l'empire Sassanide, I–II," *Res Orientales* 16 (2004): 141–69, and 17 (2007): 81–102.

———, "Peines et supplices dans les actes des martyrs persans et droit sassanide: nouvelles prospections," *Studia Iranica* 33 (2004): 243–69.

———, "La minorité chrétienne 'grecque' en terre d'Iran à l'époque sassanide," in *Chrétiens en terre d'Iran*, ed. R. Gyselen (Studia Iranica 33, 2006), 105–42.

Jullien, C. and F., "Le christianisme à Suse et en Susiane," *Dictionnaire de la Bible, Supplément*, fasc. 74 (2003): 596–620.

Jullien, F., "Un exemple de rélecture des origines dans l'Église syro-orientale: Théocrite et l'évêché de Shahrgard," in *Ancient and Middle Iranian Studies*, ed. A. Panaino and A. Piras (Milan, 2006), 553–60.

Labourt, J., *Le christianisme dans l'empire perse sous la dynastie sassanide* (Paris, 1904), 43–82, 104–30.

Mercier, R., "The dates in Syriac Martyr Acts," *AB* 117 (1999): 47–66.

Mosig-Walburg, K., "Die Christenverfolgung Schapurs II vor dem Hintergrund des persisch-römischen Krieges," in *Inkulturation des Christentums im Sasanidenreich*, ed. A. Mustafa, J. Tubach and G. S. Vashalomidze (Wiesbaden, 2007), 171–86.

Panaino, A., "La chiesa di Persia e l'impero sasanide. Conflitto e integrazione," in *Cristianità d'occidente e cristianità d'oriente* (Settimane di Studio, Centro Italiano di Studi sull'Alto Medievo 51; Spoleto, 2004), I, 765–863.

_____, "References to the term Yasht and other Mazdean elements in the Syriac and Greek martyrologia," in *Ancient and Middle Iranian Studies*, ed. A. Panaino and A. Piras (Milan, 2006), 167–82.

Peeters, P., "Le Passionaire d'Adiabene," *AB* 43 (1925): 261–304.

_____, "La date du martyre de S. Syméon, archevêque de Séleucie-Ctésiphon," *AB* 56 (1938): 118–43.

_____, *Le tréfonds oriental dans l'hagiographie byzantine* (Subsidia Hagiographica 26; Bruxelles, 1950).

Rist, J., "Die Verfolgung der Christen im spätantiken Sasanidenreich," *Oriens Christianus* 80 (1996): 17–42.

Schrier, O. J., "The Roman-Persian war of 421–42 in the light of Syriac evidence," *Greek, Roman and Byzantine Studies* 33 (1992): 75–82.

Schwaigert, W., *Das Christentum in Huzistan im Rahmen der frühen Kirchengeschichte Persiens bis zur Synode von Seleukeia-Ktesiphon im Jahre 410* (Diss. Marburg/Lahn, 1989).

Stern, S., "Near Eastern lunar calendars in the Syriac Martyr Acts," *Le Muséon* 117 (2004): 447–72.

van Esbroeck, M., "Abraham le Confesseur (5 s.), traducteur des martyrs perses," *AB* 95 (1977): 169–79.

van Rompay, L., "Impetuous martyrs? The situation of the Persian Christians in the last years of Yazdgard I (419–420)," in *Martyrium in Multidisciplinary Perspective*, ed. M. Lamberigts and P. van Deun (Bibliotheca Ephemeridum Theologicarum Lovaniensium 117; Louvain, 1995), 363–75.

Wiessner, G., *Zur Märtyrerüberlieferung aus der Christenverfolgung Schapurs II* (Abhandlungen der Akademie der Wissenschaften in Göttingen, phil.-hist. Kl. III.67; Göttingen, 1967). (See also the review by S. P. Brock in *Journal of Theological Studies* 19 [1968]: 300–309).

INDEXES TO THE APPENDIX

The following indexes (1)–(3) cover all the Syriac Acts of Persian Martyrs. Numbers in heavy type within square brackets denote the numbered texts in the list of Syriac texts in the first section of the Appendix.

The texts published by Bedjan in *AMS* I, II and IV, and in his *Histoire de Mar Jahbalaha* (i.e. Aba, Grigor, Yazdpaneh and Giwargis), are cited by page, and this also applies to Chabot's edition of Isho'sabran. References to PS are by column number (cols 715–778 = Shem'on A; 779–959 = Shem'on B), while those to Ma'in and to Qardag are by section number (for the former, in the edition above; for the latter, in Abbeloos's edition and Walker's English translation).

Names are normally given with the vocalization provided by Bedjan, even though in the case of Iranian names this often goes against the correct Middle Iranian forms; for these, reference should be made to Ph. Gignoux, *Noms propres sassanides en moyen-perse épigraphique* (Iranisches Personennamenbuch II: Mitteliranisches Personennamen 2; Österreichisches Akademie der Wissenschaften, Wien, 1986), with *Supplément (1986–2001)* (Mitteliranisches Personennamen 3, Öst. Ak. der Wiss., Wien, 2003).

(1) PERSONAL NAMES, EXCLUDING BIBLICAL

(bp = bishop, cath = catholicos, conf = confessor, dcn = deacon, k = king, m = martyr, metr = metropolitan, mon = monastery, mt = mountain, pr = priest, r = river, t = town, v = village)

(2) BIBLICAL PERSONAL NAMES

(3) PLACE NAMES (ALPHABETICIZED ACCORDING TO THE SYRIAC ALPHABET)

alaph

beth

gamal

dalath

he

zayin

nun

semkath

‘e

Pe

sadhe

qoph

resh

(4) NAMES OF PERSIAN MARTYRS LISTED AT THE END OF BRITISH LIBRARY, ADD. 12,150 (COPIED IN EDESSA AND DATED NOVEMBER, AD 411)

(The following list is based on the edition by F. Nau in PO 10, but it also includes a few further names preserved in Deir al-Surian Fragment 27)

Abba "first confessor"
'Abda dcn
'Abdalaha sub dcn from Seleucia-Ctesiphon
'Abdisho' pr of Maḥoze
'Abdisho' dcn
'Abdisho' dcn
'Abdisho' dcn
'Abdisho' dcn
'Abdzakya pr from B. Huzaye
'Abhaykla pr of Seleucia-Ctesiphon
Abraham bp of Arbela
Abraham pr from B. Garmai
Abraham pr from B. Huzaye
Abraham pr from Sleq
Abu pr from B. Garmai

Abursan "earlier"
Adda sub dcn
Addai pr from Sleq
Addai dcn
Addai layman
Aha sub dcn from Seleucia-Ctesiphon
Aitamar pr from Ḥadyab
Amarya dcn
Andreos pr from B. Huzaye
Andreos pr from B. Huzaye
Aphrahaṭ "earlier"
Ashpaz sub dcn from Seleucia-Ctesiphon
Azad layman
Azad layman
'STHR layman
Badboy pr of Seleucia-Ctesiphon
Badma pr of Seleucia-Ctesiphon
Bar'abda bp of Prat-Maishan
Baras pr from B. Garmai
Barba'shmin bp of Seleucia-Ctesiphon
Bardayṣan layman
Bardayza layman
Barḥabshabba pr of Maḥoze
Barḥabshabba pr from B. Huzaye
Barḥabshabba pr from Ḥadyab
Biba pr of Ḥulsar
Bulḥa "earlier"
Bolida' bp of Prat-Maishan
Candida from Meshkene
Dadaq dcn
Dali "second confessor"
Gadihab bp of Beth Lapaṭ
GNY layman
Guhshtazad layman
Hablaha pr of Seleucia-Ctesiphon
Hablaha dcn
Ḥanina pr of Seleucia-Ctesiphon
Ḥazat "earlier"
Ḥelmin dcn of Meshkene
Hudbar layman
Hormizd pr of Seleucia-Ctesiphon
Hurman bp of Ḥalwan
HLM sub dcn from Karka d-B. Slok
ḤYWN (f)
Isaac pr of Seleucia-Ctesiphon
Isaac pr of Ḥulsar
Isaac pr from Sleq
Isaac dcn
Isaac dcn
Isaac sub dcn
Jacob pr from Sleq
Jacob pr from Telta Shalila
Jacob dcn
Joseph pr from Beth Huzaye
Kabsin dcn of Meshkene
Kasri layman
Kosru dcn
Longinus pr of Meshkene
Madyan dcn of Meshkene
Malki dcn
Mari pr of Ḥulsar
Mari pr from Sleq
Mari dcn
Mari dcn
Marsan pr from Ḥadyab
Marya dcn
Maryab sub dcn from Ardashir
Maṭron (f)
Mela dcn
Menophilus "earlier"
Milos bp "earlier"
Nqib Edna pr of Seleucia-Ctesiphon
Nqib Edna pr from B. Huzaye
Nqib Edna sub dcn
Nqib Edna bar qyama
Narsa bp of Shaharqart
Narsa layman
Nukria pr from Sleq
Pambaq pr from B. Garmai
Papa pr from B. Garmai
Papa pr of Ḥulsar
Papa pr from Ḥadyab
Papa dcn of Meshkene
Papon layman
Paul bp of Kashkar

Paul pr of Seleucia-Ctesiphon
Paul pr of Seleucia-Ctesiphon
Paul sub dcn from Seleucia-Ctesiphon
Peter pr from B. Garmai
Pusiq layman
Qabugbed layman
Qayoma pr of Seleucia-Ctesiphon
Riyashdar dcn of Meshkene
Ṣarifa pr from Sleq
Sasan pr from B. Garmai
Sasan
Sasi dcn
Saṭra pr from Sleq
Sebina bp of Beth Lapaṭ
Shabor bp of Karka d-Beth Slok
Shahdost bp of Seleucia-Ctesiphon
Shalum
Shem'on bar Ṣabb'e bp of Seleucia-Ctesiphon
Shem'on pr of Ḥulsar
Shem'on pr from B. Huzaye
Shila pr of Maḥoze
Sinai "earlier"
Susi pr from B. Garmai
Thekla bat qyama from K. d-B. Slok
Tiray pr of Maḥoze
Tiray layman
TRN layman
Wadan dcn of Meshkene
Walash layman
Yamnosh (f)
Yazdandukt bat qyama from Karka d-B. Slok
Yoḥannan bp of Arbela
Yoḥannan bp of Hormizd Ardashir
Yoḥannan pr from B. Huzaye
Yoḥannan bp of Karka d-Beth Slok
Yoḥannan bp of Prat Maishan
Yoḥanna dcn
Yoḥannan layman
Zizi pr of Seleucia-Ctesiphon.